UNDERSTANDING

UNDERSTANDING

ELIMINATING STRESS AND DISSATISFACTION IN LIFE AND RELATIONSHIPS

JANE NELSEN, Ed.D

SUNRISE PRESS
4984 Arboleda Drive
Fair Oaks, California 95628

Understanding: Eliminating Stress
And Dissatisfaction
In Life and Relationships

Cover Design by David Anderson
Cover Photograph by Tom Myers, Sacramento, CA
Printed by Spilman Printing Co., Sacramento, CA

Library of Congress catalog card number: 85-63353

ISBN: 0-9606896-2-1

This book is lovingly dedicated to my children

Terry
Jim
Ken
Brad
Lisa
Mark
and Mary

with the hope that they enjoy the buried treasure within much
sooner than I did.

TABLE OF CONTENTS

ACKNOWLEDGMENTS

I was once a *workshop junkie*. I used to jokingly wonder if I would ever find *the last workshop* -- a workshop that would finally teach me *the magic techniques* that would give me enough competence and confidence to be truly helpful to myself and others. I never found what I was looking for. I found something better -- principles that taught me where competence, confidence, and wisdom are and always have been -- within myself.

The intellectual knowledge that "the kingdom of heaven is within" was not new to me, but I had never *experienced* this truth. I finally discovered a seminar where principles were explained that led me to *experience* my inner kingdom of happiness and peace of mind. I gratefully acknowledge and give thanks to George Pransky and Robert Kausen of the Life Education Institute in San Rafael, California. They put up with my "what ifs" and "yes buts" until I was finally able to **hear** at a deeper level.

The principles that led to my experience of inner peace and wisdom have been formulated into a new and revolutionary psychology by Enrique M. Suarez, Ph.D., and Roger C. Mills, Ph.D. These principles are now referred to as The Psychology of Mind.[1] The Psychology of Mind represents a major breakthrough in the understanding of psychological functioning.

After experiencing such dramatic results in my own life, I felt inspired to spend six months in fellowship at the Advanced Human Studies Institute in Coral Gales, Florida. Studying and working with Dr. Enrique M. Suarez and Dr. Kimberly Kiddoo was truly a beautiful and enriching exper-

---

[1] *Sanity, Insanity and Common Sense: The Missing Link in Understanding Mental Health* by Enrique M. Suarez, Ph.D., and Roger C. Mills, Ph.D.

xi

ience. What a privilege to be led to a deeper understanding of inner resources via the wisdom of these pioneers and innovators in this new psychology. I also had the privilege of working with clients at the Institute and witnessed the outstanding results. People with every imaginable mental dysfunction were able to change dramatically after internalizing the Psychology of Mind principles .

Syd Banks provided the initial inspiration. I am grateful for the opportunities I have had to attend his lectures and experience his wisdom and good feelings. Every time I read his book, Second Chance,[2] I experience deeper understanding.

I am especially grateful to by husband Barry, and my children to whom this book is dedicated. We continually love and learn from each other. I recently got lost, for a short time, in feelings of insecurity and was behaving irrationally. My ten-year-old daughter, Mary, later said, "I knew you would soon realize what you were doing, Mom."

---

[2]*Second Chance* by Syd Banks

FOREWORD

It has always been apparent to me that the role of any science or profession is to make life easier for the ordinary human being. What good is a scientific development that does not have practical application in a human being's day to day life? The fact is that people need answers for every day living.

As a practicing psychologist, I had always given my patients the best I knew. My best was, for the most part, not good enough. In 1978 I was privileged to have been part of an exciting new development in the field of psychology that has since come to be referred to as The Psychology of Mind. This new understanding has begun to change not only the manner in which professionals assist people, but also the results of this assistance.

A new development in psychology is not the end of the line, but the beginning. When the principles of the Psychology of Mind became apparent to me, it also became apparent that this new understanding would be introduced into the various fields, as well as to the public, by professionals who would have to first begin to understand it for themselves. Dr. Nelsen is one of these professionals.

This book is valuable for several reasons:

First, it is making available to the general public a readable account of a recent development in psychology that up to now has been pretty much restricted to professional circles.

Second, it redirects the individual to look within themselves for the answers to their every day emotional

xiii

problems, rather than outside themselves, as has traditionally been the practice. This is no small contribution.

Third, it is pointing people to recognize that understanding is something deeper and more fundamental than thinking.

I feel that Dr. Nelsen has contributed a most needed book that will begin to help people find more *common sensical* ways of living a healthy and happy life. The most beautiful aspect of Dr. Nelsen's *Understanding* is that it is pointing the reader, in a multitude of ways, to realize that all mental and emotional resources required for living are already resident within the individual, and that when these resources emerge they do so in the form of positive feelings and emotions.

So, while many today expound the virtues of marriage, family, and interpersonal relationships as being integral in realizing one's love and happiness, too few have recognized which comes first; which is the horse and which is the cart. Dr. Nelsen has beautifully outlined for the reader the fact that the feeling of love and happiness is a resource within ourselves, and is the principle ingredient that goes into marriage and family life -- indeed every facet of our daily activity. This is a precious recognition, without which the search for contentment and happiness via marriage, family, or relationships is bound for failure.

In my view, Dr. Nelsen has successfully presented a version of the principles of the Psychology of Mind in a manner that is practical and understandable. Her contribution will no doubt have a significant impact on the manner in which the general public presently views psychological advice.

Finally, Dr. Nelsen's contribution to each individual reading the book is priceless, pointing the way to a life of greater happiness and mental health.

Enrique M. Suarez, Ph.D.
Executive Director
Advanced Human Studies Institute
Coral Gables, Florida

PART ONE

SECRETS TO HAPPINESS

AND

PEACE OF MIND

Chapter 1

A TREASURE MAP

Everyone is looking for answers that will help them find happiness and peace of mind. Even though this is what everyone wants, many find that the joy in life and relationships is missing most of the time as they live in stress, anxiety, dissatisfaction, disappointment, anger, or depression.

Many words of wisdom about happiness and peace of mind are available through spoken and written words. You have probably had the experience of feeling inspired by beautiful words of wisdom and vowed *to be better*, but found it difficult to maintain those inspired feelings.

Perhaps you have found that sometimes, even when you could remember what you *should do*, you just didn't feel able to do it. You may have had times when you felt like giving up with feelings of discouragement, failure, and self-blame. Then you may have felt inspired to do better again -- only to repeat the cycle.

What does it take to *understand* words of wisdom so that they are integrated into your being at such a deep level that it becomes natural and easy to live in joy and harmony? How can you maintain those feelings of inspiration so that words of wisdom are truly helpful in your life, rather than becoming just more *shoulds* that you feel you can't live up to.

This book will explain four principles which can show you how to accomplish this. These principles of psychological functioning have been formulated into the new Psychology of Mind by Enrique M. Suarez. Ph.D. and Roger C. Mills, Ph.D.,[*] and are discussed in chapters three, four, five, and six. Once you *understand* these princi-

---

[*]*Sanity, Insanity and Common Sense, The Missing Link in Under-standing Mental Health* by E. M. Suarez, Ph.D. and Roger C. Mills, Ph.D.

ples, you will find the treasure that is buried deep within you.

Living with peace of mind and happiness comes from beautiful feelings which are inherently within each of us. We learn unnatural processes to keep these feelings buried. When they are uncovered we live naturally in a happy, loving state of mind. The kingdom of heaven *is* within.

An *understanding* of the four principles is like a treasure map which will show you how to uncover your natural feelings of love and appreciation for the beauty of life. With these feelings it becomes effortless to live in happiness and peace of mind. When these feelings are uncovered you will find you have natural access to your common sense and wisdom. And, whatever you do from your own common sense and wisdom, will provide joy, ease, and happiness in your life and your relationships.

How can I make such claims? Because an *understanding* of the principles has worked so beautifully in my own life, and in the lives of friends, clients, and other therapists who have come to *understand* them.

Words of wisdom now have meaning for me at a deep enough level to make them obvious rather than an effort to follow.

This does not mean I never get *off course* into unhappiness, but the principles show me exactly how I get *off course* and point me back in the direction of my natural good feelings. Like any map that is used often, the course soon becomes so natural that it is easy to find the way without the map -- without even thinking about it.

Teachers of the principles explained in this book have first found happiness and peace of mind in their own lives. They then experience the added pleasure of watching it work in the lives of their clients and students.

I was once like many therapists who are sincerely trying to help people, while their own lives are filled with varying degrees of stress, anxiety, dissatisfaction, feelings of inadequacy, depression, or other forms of insecurity.

This is not meant as a criticism of therapists, whose primary motivation is to help people. The problem is that many of us have been well trained in effective *coping skills*. This can be very helpful, because coping is certainly better than not coping. However, it only brings temporary relief, until the next problem is encountered. Coping is like bailing water when we don't know how to plug the hole in the boat. Bailing is much better than sinking.

The exciting news is that the principles in this book show us how to plug the hole. We don't need to learn how to cope with stress or other forms of insecurity. We can eliminate them. Many examples of common *problem situations* in life and relationships will be given in later chapters, showing how the *problem* is eliminated through *understanding*.

Can you imagine what life would be like without problems? I remember being concerned that peace of mind would be boring. What a silly notion. Happiness and peace of mind are great treasures. *Understanding* is the *treasure map*.

Someone once asked, "So, what is the point of all this?"

My answer, "To be happy."

You already know how to be happy. That is one well kept secret. An *understanding* of the principles can uncover your natural knowledge and abilities, which are so easy to *lose sight of* in our present social structure.

This treasure map to *understanding* is the most valuable gift I have ever found. It has helped me see that I already had everything I ever wanted. I could not **see** the good feelings and happiness buried deep within myself much of the time because I kept looking for them elsewhere. I often missed **seeing** what I had when I turned my back and headed away from life instead of embracing life.

My life was once based on feelings of insecurity. This would have surprised many, if they had known, because I was very good at achieving all the things people commonly search for in their quest for happiness. Since my search was based on illusions of insecurity, none of these things kept me happy for long. It was important to me that I *appeared* secure as another way of trying to keep those feelings of insecurity hidden. It didn't work. The insecure feelings were like a foundation of quicksand waiting to swallow me every time *I thought* I was failing, or if I rested for very long *on my laurels* before trying to achieve more *success*.

The tables have been turned. I used to be happy about 20% of the time. The other 80% was spent trying to escape the quicksand of the illusions of insecurity.

I am now happy 80% of the time. The 20% detours into unhappiness have lost intensity and longevity. Actually, what I once thought was unhappiness no longer feels like unhappiness when not taken seriously.

When I uncovered the natural happiness within myself I could then truly enjoy and appreciate all that life has to offer -- all that I once took for granted. What I once thought I didn't have no longer matters. It is impossible to feel satisfaction and *want* at the same time.

My life is filled with feelings of security and peace of mind. I now have a compass which lets me know when I get off course and keeps me headed in a direction toward deeper understanding.

My search is over. I have found the buried treasure within myself. You can find it too.

Happy treasure hunt!

Chapter 2

LISTENING SOFTLY

As you read this book, listen softly. Listen from your heart for a feeling within that lets you hear truth. Of course, I don't mean literally from your heart. That is simply the closest I can come with words to explain the experience of insight or realization from within.

Learning from insight or realization is much different than learning from the intellect. The brain has unlimited capacity and capabilities, but most of us have limited our brains with a thought system which has been *programed* with concepts, interpretations, and beliefs. This programed thought system has a difficult time computing anything new. The *program* wants to fit everything into what it already knows -- or to reject it.

Listen softly for a feeling, because words are inadequate to express love, beauty, principle, or any other truth. These truths can be understood only through the personal experience of them, which is beyond words.

We often focus on words and miss the feeling being expressed. Each person hears words from their own frame of reference and interpretations. The picture of a dog that you carry in your mind will be different from that of all your friends who loved a different kind of dog. There are many words which evoke stronger beliefs and reactions from our individual thought systems than the word dog.

Listening softly helps us get past the limitation of words. Words sound so hollow. The experience of what the words are trying to convey is so full. The gap between the two is bridged by the *understanding* that comes from insight.

When you listen for a feeling, you will know what is meant in spite of misused words. You will probably even know (from your own inspiration) another way to explain principles of truth that will make more sense to you.

Any principle can be difficult to learn unless we bypass our limited thought systems so we can experience *insight*. The principles, which will soon be explained, help us remember how to bypass our limited thought systems. I say remember, because we were born with that capability, and used it as children to enjoy life, and to learn, and to experience many beautiful things. Insight is a recognition of the obvious. The obvious often eludes us when we are stuck in our programed thought systems.

Remember when you were trying to learn math principles? At first it did not matter how many times you added 2 + 2; it didn't really make sense. Then, suddenly you *caught on*, and you could add any combination of numbers. It made sense that 5 + 7 was the same as 7 + 5. This is one example of insight.

Learning to ride a bicycle is another example. No matter how many times we heard an explanation of balance, it was beyond our comprehension until we had the experience of balance.

We kept plugging away at math and practicing balance, even when the principles did not make sense to us. We had faith that we would eventually learn and be able to produce all kinds of good results with these abilities. Some of us may have practiced out of love for the teacher rather than faith in future results. Others may have developed a belief that they could not do it and may still have *blocks* about math or balance.

The principles of math and balance do not provide answers. They simply show us how to find answers or how to discover mistakes and make corrections. The principles explained in this book show us how to find answers and make corrections in our lives.

Reading this book could be like a puzzle. Sometimes one piece of a puzzle does not make sense until it fits with another piece. It could be that something you read in the middle or at the end will give you insight that will make the beginning more understandable.

This book is short so that it will be easy to read many times. If you get even a glimmer of *insight,* you will get more each time you read. Your reading experience will be different as your *understanding* deepens. When your *understanding* is deep enough, it will automatically overide your limited, programed thought system and keep you in touch with your own wisdom.

As you read, let yourself have fun noticing how difficult it can be to *hear* and *understand* the principles when you use your programed thought system -- that intellectual process which blocks common sense, wisdom, and inspiration.

Most of your questions will be answered as you keep reading. The answers will not come from what you read, but from insight from your own common sense and wisdom. The purpose of this book is to help you regain greater access to these sources within yourself.

Understanding is the key to natural happiness and peace of mind.

Listening for a feeling is the key to insight.

Insight is the key to understanding.

This is the cycle. It does not matter where you start. They all lead in the same direction for positive results in your life and relationships.

You are reading this book because of your hope that you will be able to achieve the promised results of joy, contentment, happiness, and peace of mind. Like math and balance, before understanding, principles can seem complicated. After understanding, they seem beautifully simple.

When you catch on to the upcoming principles with insight, you will *experience beautiful results in your life.*

Keep listening softly.

Chapter 3

THE PRINCIPLE OF THINKING AS A FUNCTION

You think! This is the best kept secret of all.

Understanding that you think is the key to understanding everything else in life.

You may be saying, "That is not a secret. Everyone knows that they think."

Actually, very few people know that they think. They believe they are the victims of their thoughts, rather than the producers of their thoughts. Instead of knowing that thinking is a function or an ability, they believe what they think is reality.

Thinking is something we do to create our reality, rather than reality being something that is reflected in our thoughts. Thoughts come from the inside out, not from the outside in. We can think *anything* we choose to think. Our emotions are then a direct result of what we choose to think. Any form of insecurity, stress, or anxiety is a direct result of believing thoughts are *reality* rather than products of our thinking ability.

As soon as you take the content of your thoughts seriously, you have forgotten that you think.

Joe feels inadequate. He believes his inadequacy is real. He doesn't know that it is just a thought. His inadequacy cannot exist unless he thinks it; but because he believes it is real, he bases his behavior on that thought and acts inadequate.

Melissa is depressed. She believes she is depressed because life is overwhelming. Life cannot be overwhelming. Only what she thinks about life makes it feel overwhelming.

Archie Bunker is a bigot. He thinks other people are inferior. He believes his thoughts are reality, not just thoughts.

25

Anyone who believes their thoughts are reality has forgotten that they think and that they can think literally anything they want. They have forgotten that when they change their thoughts, their reality changes.

It is very simple. If you don't like what you are thinking about, stop thinking about it.

You may argue, "How can I possibly stop thinking about what I am thinking about? I have tried that, and it didn't work."

You keep thinking certain thoughts only when you believe they are reality and take them seriously. When you stop taking them seriously, it takes effort to keep thinking about them.

Understanding that you think makes it difficult to take any of your negative thoughts seriously.

Taking your negative thoughts seriously, simply means you have forgotten that you can think anything you want.

THINKING FROM A CLEAR CHANNEL OR FROM A PROGRAMED THOUGHT SYSTEM

Everyone has a thought system where they store all the memories, perceptions, judgments, and beliefs that make up the filters it takes to create each person's unique, separate reality. (Separate realities is discussed further in Chapter 5.)

Everyone also has a clear channel through which they can experience common sense, wisdom, inspiration, and all the good feelings that are naturally inherent in every human being.

We experience life differently through our clear channel than we do through our thought system. Through our clear channel we see life freshly, moment to moment. Through our thought system, we see only our beliefs about life, just like Archie Bunker does.

When we take thoughts from our thought system seriously, we clog our clear channel and lose access to common sense and wisdom. Our natural good feelings cannot get through because they are blocked by the garbage of our thought system.

We start creating a thought system when we are very young. It is made up of our own perceptions and interpretations and the thoughts and interpretations we accept from others.

We are very trusting when we are young. We usually believe what anyone tells us. Unfortunately, much of what we are told is *garbage* being passed along from generation to generation. This is not done maliciously. Our family and friends would not pass on troublesome beliefs if they knew what they were doing. They accepted beliefs that were passed on to them when they were young because they did not know any better.

Most of these beliefs are full of *shoulds* and *shouldn'ts* that contain judgments of worth or worthlessness. We are told how we should be in order to be liked and to be successful. We are also told how others should be and how life should be. We, others, and life, hardly ever fit these beliefs; so we live in failure, pseudo success, anxiety, stress, or disappointment in ourselves, life, and others.

Our thought system also contains helpful information and skills such as reading, writing, arithmetic, names, phone numbers, and other knowledge that makes life easier and more enjoyable. This information is factual and does not create emotions. We use it for our benefit rather than against ourselves.

It is the illusionary thoughts, which create negative emotions, that get us into trouble when we believe they are reality.

The beliefs and interpretations we accept or create can seem so real that we live and die for them, even when they do not make sense. Senseless thinking is often easier to see in other people than it is to see in ourselves.

I remember thinking schizophrenics were really crazy when they thought they saw little green bugs crawling up the wall, or believed they were Napoleon. It was obvious to me that those were crazy thoughts. But, of course, all my thoughts were serious and real -- even the ones that made me miserable.

One psychologist shares that before she had a deeper understanding of these principles, she had a client in therapy who believed a garbage truck was going to eat her.

The psychologist spontaneously laughed and said, "That is a silly thought." She had spoken from her common sense and wisdom but felt a little embarrassed because in her

27

training she had learned it is not appropriate to laugh at something a client is taking seriously.

Fortunately, the client *heard* the truth of those words at an even deeper level than they had been spoken. She improved significantly after that. Several months later the psychologist asked her what had made the difference in her recovery.

The client replied, "It was the day you told me my thoughts couldn't hurt me."

We all have silly thoughts which we take seriously. When we know they are just thoughts, they can't hurt us. They will not have power over us, especially the negative ones which make our lives miserable. We will remember that we have power over our thoughts.

Another client quit having panic attacks after hearing the above story. She said, "The last time a panic attack started, I knew it was just my thoughts. I laughed, and felt fine."

I know it is not this simple for everyone. It wasn't for me. Some people *understand* sooner than others.

No one wants the misery which is created by negative thoughts. Some people seem to live as though they do, but that is because they do not understand the difference between thinking through their clear channel and thinking through their programed thought system.

The next time you are feeling upset or miserable, notice what you are thinking. Your emotions are created by your thoughts.

When we *realize* that thinking is a function or an ability rather than a reality, we can easily dismiss the negative thoughts we create and keep the channel clear to express our natural, good feelings. The first thing common sense and wisdom let us **see** is how funny it is to take negative thoughts seriously and base our lives on them.

Many have argued, "Good feelings are not natural to me. It is more natural for me to feel stress or depressed. I don't try to feel these things; they are just naturally there."

They are not just naturally there. There is a negative thought behind every negative feeling.

Can you imagine the problems babies and young children would have if they tried to learn to walk and talk through insecurities produced by a programed thought system. The first thing most of them would *think* is that they could not possibly accomplish these great tasks, and their progress would stop.

When we rediscover that childlike quality of not thinking through a programed thought system, our life becomes as much fun as a child's. We lose all forms of insecurity and each day is full of wonder, adventure, and delight in all there is to experience in life.

If it seems that I am going on and on about this principle, it is because I am. I know this can be the most difficult one to understand, because most people try to figure it out from their programed thought system. The filters of the thought system created the distortions in the first place, so it is impossible to see things differently while using that same thought system.

I am saying the same thing over and over in different ways, hoping that one of the ways will sneak past your filters and reach your common sense and wisdom where all great discoveries and new learning takes place.

Looking at life through our programed thought system is the same as looking at the world through *extremely dark* glasses labeled judgment, blame, expectations, pride, ego, anger, shoulds, and other forms of insecurity based on thought. These glasses are like blinders and filters which distort our view of life. The distortion becomes our reality and shuts out everything else, including the truth.

Are you wondering, "What is the truth?"

The truth is what you see when you take off the dark glasses (dismiss negative thoughts.)

Whenever we have any negative feelings, we can be aware of the fact that we are wearing one of our pairs of ugly, dark glasses (our thought system). As soon as we take them off (dismiss our thoughts) we see with greater perspective and our reality changes.

Sometimes those dark glasses may feel stuck on with super glue, and it may seem as though you can't get them off for a while. You feel *stuck in your thought system.* Knowing what is happening, even when we can't seem to get out of it, shortens the *stuckness* tremendously. It is only *thinking* about our stuckness, and taking it seriously, that allows it to hang on and get worse.

When first learning about thought, many people find themselves in variations of the following four states of thought:

FOUR STATES OF THOUGHT

1. Being caught up in thoughts and *taking them seriously.*
2. Being caught up in thoughts, but not taking them quite as seriously because of an *understanding* that they are just thoughts.
3. Being at rest. Dismissing thoughts and getting quiet to clear the channel for inspiration and insight.
4. Inspiration -- when our clear channel is being used to express wisdom and common sense.

We usually go in and out of variations of these states of thought many times a day. *Understanding* the principles simply lets us know what is happening, and thus shortens the visits to states one and two.

When we understand our programed thought system for the filter that it is, we will be able to bypass it, except for occasional, short visits. When we understand what happens when we are there, we won't want to stay for long. Each visit will simply confirm that thinking through our thought system does not produce happiness and peace of mind (unless we are using it to remember useful facts and skills).

At this point or sooner, many people get the notion that thinking is *the bad guy* and we should not think. Thinking is a beautiful gift through which we experience the beauty of life.

We are almost always thinking. *Understanding* makes it natural to dismiss negative thoughts which come from our programed thought system and to enjoy a nice life through our clear channel.

The key is to know where our thoughts are coming from.

The next principle gives us the key.

Chapter 4

THE PRINCIPLE OF FEELINGS AS A COMPASS

Our feelings are like a compass which lets us know where we are on our treasure map. When we are feeling good, we are on the right course, through our clear channels, to find happiness and peace of mind in life. When we are feeling bad, we are off course into our thought systems.

Remember, it is impossible to have negative feelings without thoughts from your thought system. Thus, negative feelings are the compass which lets you know you are thinking from your thought system.

Negative feelings let us know it is time to dismiss negative thoughts. Positive feelings let us know we are experiencing life through our clear channel where we have access to our natural good feelings.

Good feelings are like corks which naturally bob to the top of water unless they are weighted down. Good feelings are natural in human beings unless they are weighted down with negative thoughts which are taken seriously.

When first learning about the principles, I thought *understanding* would mean I would never again *get lost* in my thought system even for short visits. I would become very disappointed in myself every time I took my thoughts seriously. I did not know that it is normal to get off course.

It was an insightful experience for me when my wisdom let me know that it did not matter that my negative thoughts kept creeping in. (They were not actually *creeping* in. We can get so proficient at instantaneously pulling up *files* from our programed thought system that we forget they are still our moment-to-moment creations. It then seems that thoughts creep into our mind beyond our control, which is impossible.) I had the experience of just watching those thoughts without judging them. I even felt a tolerant affection for my negative thoughts. When I understood they

31

were just thoughts, they could not hurt me. It was easy to laugh and dismiss them.

Everyone continually gets off course. *Understanding* just helps us not to take it seriously, not to judge ourselves, and to be open for inspiration to lead us back on course.

A word of caution: Many people claim they are just following their *feelings* when they do negative things, like *getting out* their anger, or telling another person that their judgments about them are *the truth.*

Any feelings that are negative or produce negative results come from a distorted frame of reference or programed thought system. *Feelings* from wisdom and common sense are always positive.

Positive feelings flow naturally from our clear channel. The *feeling* comes first and is then experienced through the gift of thinking. Negative feelings are experience after we create negative thoughts from our thought system. *If the feeling comes first, it is from your clear channel. If the feeling comes second, it is from your thought system.*

Soon after hearing this, I had an opportunity to experience the truth of what I am saying. During a one week seminar where I was learning more about the principles, I called home to see how my children were doing. I was informed that thirteen-year-old Mark had been suspended from school. This is how Mark told the story:

"I found some cigarettes in my locker. I don't know how they got there. I was just putting them in my pocket to take them to the principal when a teacher came by and took me to the principal."

My thoughts went crazy for a few minutes. "He is lying to us. I'm a failure as a mother. If he is smoking cigarettes, he is probably also into alcohol and drugs. He is going to ruin his life. What will people think?"

I was feeling pretty upset, so my feeling compass let me know loud and clear that I was caught up in my thought system and was not seeing things clearly. I dismisssed my compass instead of my thoughts for a minute and used more thoughts to argue with my common sense, "Yes, but this is different. These are really terrible circumstances over which I have no control. How could I possibly see them differently. I am going to have to scold Mark severely, *ground* him for at least a month, take away all his privileges, and let him know he is ruining his life."

Fortunately, I had too much faith in the principles to take those thoughts seriously. I dismissed my crazy thoughts and inspiration quickly bobbed to the top. I then saw the circumstances in a completely different way.

I felt understanding and compassion for Mark's view of the situation. He had just entered junior high school where the pressure is enormous to follow the crowd rather than common sense.

When I got home I followed my inspiration and knew what to do. I sat down with Mark, put my arm around him, and said, "Mark, I'll bet it is tough trying to figure out how to say 'no' to your friends so you won't be called a nerd or a party pooper."

Mark had been expecting my usual craziness and hardly knew how to respond to my sanity. He tentatively said, "Yeah."

I went on, "And I'll bet the only reason you would ever lie to us is because you love us so much you don't want to disappoint us."

Tears filled his eyes, and he gave me a big hug. I responded with tears in my own eyes as we experienced those wonderful feelings of love. I reassured him, "If you think you could ever disappoint us, then we are not doing a good enough job of letting you know how much we love you, unconditionally.

You can use your own imagination to guess what the results would have been if I had followed my crazy thoughts to interact with Mark. My guess is that my craziness would have inspired increased rebelliousness.

I am continually grateful for the principle of using my feelings as a compass to let me know when I am *off track*. Whenever I am feeling upset, angry, judgmental, disappointed, or any other negative feeling, I know it is all being created by thoughts which I am taking seriously. As soon as I recognize that, and dismiss the thoughts, I am filled with natural good feelings.

Dismissing negative thoughts is not the same as sticking your head in the sand. It is the same as taking off blinders and filters so the situation can be seen with perspective. Sometimes the problem disappears along with the negative thoughts. Other times the problem may still be there, but it looks and feels different. You will see solutions rather than problems. From a happy state of mind, solutions are obvious.

It is amazing how different the world seems when you dismiss negative thoughts so your natural good feelings can surface. Common sense and wisdom flow.

Chapter 5

THE PRINCIPLE OF SEPARATE REALITIES

Another well kept secret is the fact that everyone lives in a separate reality. This simply means that we all *interpret* things differently.

You may object, "That is not a secret. Everyone knows that."

It is true that most of us have heard about this principle. A popular example is that everyone who sees an accident describes it differently. The explanation is obvious when we *understand* that everyone sees through the filters of their own, unique thought systems.

Hearing about separate realities, however, and *understanding* the principle at a deep level are not the same. When we really *understand* the fact of separate realities, we will stop spending so much time and energy trying to change the reality of others.

We have separate realities because everyone has a different thought system made up of individually unique memories, interpretations and beliefs. These memories, interpretations and beliefs act as filters through which present events are seen. These filters make it impossible to see what IS with fresh perspective.

Without *understanding* we become unaware of our filters and think that our interpretations are real. We become convinced that if we try hard enough we will be able to persuade others that our reality is the *right* one. This *never works* -- so nations go to war, marriages break up, and parents and children experience a *generation gap*.

The reverse can also apply. Some people think their reality is wrong or not as good as others. They spend a lot of time feeling inadequate, insecure, and depressed.

"But some things really are wrong!" you may argue.

With *understanding*, we see that this need not be an issue. Everyone does the best they can with what they know. We are much happier when we see the innocence in all behavior and feel compassion or interest rather than judgment. When we have *understanding* it is natural to, "Forgive them, for they know not what they do."

When we don't understand separate realities, we have thoughts like, "How could they possibly be like that, or do that? They would be happier if they would do it my way, like my kind of music (especially at the volume I prefer), eat the foods I like, and load the dishwasher the way I do."

We usually understand separate realities when visiting another country. We could not enjoy traveling if we told people of other countries they should speak our language and change all their customs. Traveling is enjoyable when we learn all we can about differences and find them fascinating.

Phil and Lisa experienced separate realities soon after they were married. Phil was an *early bird*. He loved getting up at the crack of dawn full of energy and ready to enjoy the day. Every morning he would bounce out of bed, and sing loudly in the shower, hoping Lisa would wake up. Noticing Lisa still in bed with the covers pulled over her head, he would noisily bounce on the bed as he put on his shoes and socks, thinking, "If she really loved me, she would get up and enjoy this time with me."

Lisa, totally annoyed at what she saw as *his inconsiderateness*, would be thinking, "If he really loved me, he would know I hate getting up early and would be quiet and let me sleep."

They would discuss their differences often, but neither really *heard* the other because they were more interested in changing each other than in understanding each other.

Christmas was a disaster. When Lisa was growing up, everyone in her family had received one very nice, expensive present for Christmas. In Phil's family everyone had enjoyed the fun of opening a whole bunch of inexpensive presents. So, Lisa would buy Phil one nice, expensive present. Phil would buy Lisa a whole bunch of inexpensive presents. Every Christmas they would feel disappointed and misunderstood. They each thought the other was too dense to know how to *really* enjoy Christmas.

We can laugh at how foolish Phil and Lisa are for not seeing how simple it would be to solve their problem by respecting their separate realities instead of trying to change each other. However, we often become just as blind when it comes to our own precious beliefs.

Our world expands greatly when we *understand* and appreciate separate realities. It is then possible to enjoy differences (or at least understand them) instead of fighting over them.

When we quit seeing separate realities as right or wrong, we see ourselves and others without judgment. This is really nice because we are not left with all those negative feelings we are stuck with when we are being judgmental. People who insist that it is important for them to be judgmental so they can keep the world from going to *hell*, find that they live most of their lives in *hell,* which does not help the world.

Have you noticed how important it *seems* to tell others when we think they are *wrong,* especially those we love? Then we wonder why they don't appreciate it.

Dan used to dread visiting his father because they would always end up with bad feelings. Dan shared, "We used to spend all our time together arguing about who was right and who was wrong. I was certainly never going to admit I was wrong because it seemed very clear to me that I wasn't. Dad would not admit he was wrong, even though I made every effort to let him know how old fashioned his ideas were. Understanding separate realities was a Godsend for me. Dad and I no longer argue over our differences. I respect how he sees things and know I would see them the same way if I were in his shoes. Now we just share the love and gratitude we have and enjoy each other's company."

It is not helpful to judge your own reality either. One day I was judging myself for not having a deeper *understanding* of the principles. I suddenly *realized* that any form of judgment would only block my understanding. When I stopped judging my present reality, I could see that to say I should be farther along than I am, or that someone else should have a different reality than they do, makes as much sense as saying a rosebud should be a rose in full bloom.

Every human being is in the process of evolving, learning, and changing in awareness of what life is all about. Getting in the way with our judgments only creates negativity and impedes progress. Can you imagine how much more helpful we would be to ourselves and others if we were loving and compassionate instead of judgmental?

A master gardener does not fret and fume because his roses are not growing into petunias. He simply nurtures all of his flowers with water, weeding, and fertilizer so they can reach their full potential as roses, petunias, begonias, or whatever they are. We can likewise simply enjoy and nurture who we and others are rather than destroying our natural capacity to enjoy a beautiful life that is not corrupted with *shoulds* and *oughts*.

Shoulds are not necessary when we have access to wisdom. A truly happy person could not do anything to hurt another person or himself.

Nurturing ourselves and others comes naturally when we have *understanding*. Wisdom lets us know that the **key is not to judge, but to love and nurture.**

Higher levels of understanding will come naturally from the positive feelings that surface when judgmental thoughts are dismissed.

Chapter 6

THE PRINCIPLE OF MOOD LEVELS (OR LEVELS OF CONSCIOUSNESS)

Everyone has moods. Some may *seem* to fluctuate more extremely than others, but the fact is that everyone experiences times when they feel good and times when they feel low.

Have you noticed how different your own *separate reality* is depending on whether your mood is high or low? Given the same circumstances, when you are in a high mood, you will **see** things one way. When you are in a low mood, you will **see** the same things differently.

Remember those times when you were driving along in a good mood and someone needed to cut in front of you and you cheerfully waved them in, remembering all the times you have been in the same situation. Now, remember the times you were in a low mood and you stepped on the gas, determined not to let them in, mumbling about how stupid and inconsiderate *they* were.

Higher moods or levels of consciousness simply mean that we are able to see things with more perspective and with greater understanding of the *big picture.* Lower moods or levels of consciousness simply mean that we have lost perspective and understanding.

When we are in a low mood everything looks bad. We may feel overwhelmed and have feelings of impending doom. There seems to be no way out. The grass is definitely greener somewhere else.

The secret is knowing that moods are not nearly as bad as the thoughts we have about them. It is our thoughts about low moods that make them seem really awful.

I remember when I used to get depressed. I would feel inadequate and insecure about something and would retreat into depression. Then I would be upset at myself for being depressed, and would feel more inadequate and insecure and would get more depressed. I did not understand the vicious cycle I was creating with my thoughts. Later, I started looking forward to my depressions because I would use them as an excuse to lie in bed all day and read. My depressions quit lasting very long when I started enjoying them. I finally saw the obvious and realized I did not have to get depressed in order to take a day to rest and enjoy myself. My common sense was letting me know it was time to get quiet.

A quiet mind is the best cure for a low mood. A quiet mind is what you have naturally when you dismiss thoughts from your thought system.

Sometimes the simple realization that *it is just a mood*, will be enough to raise your level of consciousness immediately. The moment this happens your thoughts will be dismissed, your mind will quiet, and you will have access to wisdom, common sense, and inspiration, and you will see things from a different perspective. Your reality will change.

Ellen was upset because a department store had not refunded her money as promised. She was taking her anger out on the customer service clerk who reacted by being rude to Ellen.

During the conversation Ellen realized what was happening. Her mood shifted immediately and she said to the clerk, "You really have a tough job, don't you?"

The clerk responded immediately, in a better mood, "I sure do." From then on she was very helpful and the problem was solved.

It all goes back to thought. In lower levels of consciousness we *react* from a thought system full of negativity. In higher levels of consciousness we *act* from inspiration, common sense, and wisdom.

It is impossible to see anything with perspective when we we are in a low mood. As soon as we see with perspective, our mood changes. It does not make sense to trust any thoughts or feelings we have in a low state of consciousness because they are being filtered through our programed thought system rather than coming from wisdom and common sense.

Understanding this principle teaches us to *get quiet* (verbally, physically, and mentally) when we are at a low level, and wait for it to pass.

NOW YOU SEE IT. NOW YOU DON'T

High or low levels of consciousness are not a matter for value or moral judgment. Consciousness is a state of awareness, perspective, or insight. Sometimes we **see** it, and sometimes we don't. The moment we recognize that we are seeing things from a lower level of consciousness, we have jumped to a higher level of consciousness. It takes perspective to realize we are not seeing something with perspective. So, the moment we recognize we have not been seeing clearly, we are **seeing** clearly. However, if in the next moment we judge ourselves because we didn't see clearly all the time, we have lost our perspective again.

When we are in a higher level of consciousness we feel love, understanding, compassion, forgiveness and gratitude. We feel satisfaction and peace of mind. We see things with greater understanding and perspective. We do not have to try to make ourselves feel these things. In a higher level of consciousness, we naturally feel them.

I can hear your question, "Yes, but what about all those times when I am not in a good mood or at a higher level of consciousness?"

Feeling bad happens, just like storms. We don't try to figure out how to stop a storm, or why it is there, or how to change it. We simply do whatever is necessary to minimize damage, make ourselves as comfortable as possible, and wait for it to pass.

A sailor knows how important it is to drop his sails when he comes into a storm. With *understanding* you will know how important it is to drop negative thoughts when you are in a low mood or have any negative feelings.

Low moods can change immediately with recognition, or they can be something like the flu and hang around even when we know what they are. When we get the flu, we know that the best thing to do is to take care of ourselves until it passes. We are also careful not to spread it around.

Sue Pettit had a wonderful insight about moods and thoughts and was inspired to write a poem entitled Lilly's

Loose. Sue was inspired by Lilly Tomlin's role as Ernestine at the switchboard and what happens when we let our thought system take over.

LILLY'S LOOSE

Lilly is the operator at the switchboard of my brain.
And when she starts reacting, my life becomes insane.
She's supposed to be employed by me
        -- and play a passive role,
But anytime I'm insecure -- Lilly takes control.

Lilly's loose, Lilly's loose, Lilly's loose today.
Tell everyone around me just to clear out of my way.
The things I say won't make much sense
        -- all common sense is lost.
'Cause when Lilly's at the switchboard
        -- my wires all get crossed.

Lilly is my own creation, thought I needed her with me
To organize and then recall all my life's history.
But she started taking liberty with all my information.
And whenever she starts plugging in
        -- I get a bad sensation.

Lilly's loose, Lilly's loose, Lilly's loose today.
Tell all my friends and relatives to clear out of my way.
I don't give hugs and kisses
        when I'm in this frame of mind.
And please don't take me seriously
        -- it'd be a waste of time.

She looks out through my eyeballs
        and sees what I do see,
Then hooks up wires to my past
        -- she thinks she's helping me!
When I'm in a good mood, I can smile at her endeavor.
But when I'm in a bad mood
        -- Lilly's boss, and is she clever.

Lilly's loose, Lilly's loose, Lilly's loose today.
Tell the world to hurry by and stay out of my way.
I'm feeling very scattered -- I'm lost in my emotion.
Lilly's on a rampage, and she's causing a commotion.

     Lilly's Loose and many other wonderful poems, which beautifully and humorously illustrate the principles of Psychology of Mind, will be published soon in a book entitled *Coming Home* by Sue Pettit .

     Understanding what low moods are makes it natural and obvious to get quiet and wait for them to pass -- or to know enough to not spread our bad moods around -- or to forgive ourselves and others when we don't have enough understanding to snap out of it or wait for it to pass.

     There are many levels of understanding.

PART TWO

PRACTICAL APPLICATION

Chapter 7

WHAT NOW?

Many people become frightened or annoyed when they first hear these principles. They are used to the habit of using their thought system to try and figure things out and can't imagine solving problems any other way. They also are used to blaming circumstances as the cause of their thinking rather than realizing it is their thinking about circumstances that creates their feelings.

Others misinterpret the principles to mean they should quit thinking and become a blob. The opposite is true. Once we truly *understand* the principles, we quit being slaves to our thought systems and thinking becomes our servant.

We will not be blobs at all. Following our common sense and wisdom, we will know what to do to create joy and ease in our lives, and wonderful relationships with others.

We rarely stop thinking, even in our sleep. This is not the point. The point is to understand that **thinking is a function** and that we have the ability to think literally anything we want to think.

Understanding helps us know when our thoughts are coming from a limited, distorted, thought system, and when our thoughts are the formulation of inspiration, common sense, and wisdom through our clear channel.

Understanding brings unlimited freedom. We need no longer be prisoners to our programed beliefs and negativity.

A misunderstanding of the principles can lead to misuse. I have often heard comments such as, "I'm afraid to ask a question, or my teacher will know I'm not very *high*."

"I still have negative thoughts, so I must not understand a thing."

47

"I'm a failure because I yelled at my children. I lost my patience and forgot to see the insecurity behind their behavior."

"I really thought I understood and would not get *caught up* in my thought system again. The very next day I let myself get hooked into negativity, just like Pavlov's dog. I felt very discouraged and disappointed in myself."

"I just can't feel compassion when my wife drinks, or my husband yells at me, or a friend disappoints me, or when things don't turn out the way I want them to. I get angry or upset."

These comments indicate a lack of deeper *understanding,* but it is not helpful to add negative judgment. When we are first learning math principles, we make mistakes. As our *understanding* grows, we make fewer mistakes or use our understanding to correct the mistakes.

Negative judgment only hampers the good feelings which encourage learning.

I once mistakenly believed that if the principles were true, I would be perfect all the time. With *understanding*, the concept of perfect and mistakes is totally different. Whenever we get upset about mistakes or *not being perfect*, we are ego involved. This simply means we have a *belief* that our self-worth is dependent upon being a certain way or having others be a certain way. Our expectations do not allow for mistakes. How silly! Life is full of *making mistakes*, if that is how you want to label some of the things we do.

Fortunately, children do not even have the concept of *mistake* when they fall down while learning to walk. *Understanding* the principles helps us recapture that childlike innocence and state of mind.

Edison was once chided, "It is too bad you had so many failures before you were successful."

Edison replied. "I didn't have any failures. I learned many things that did not work."

Principles simply give us a direction or a point of reference on our treasure map. They are also like natural laws. The natural law of gravity does not include a rule that you *should* not jump off a building. It simply explains what happens if you do. The principle of thought as a function does not include a rule that you should not think from your thought system. It simply explains what happens if you do.

Making mistakes in math is not disastrous. It does not even seem like a bother to go back over our figures to find the mistakes and correct them when we are feeling gratitude for the knowledge that allows us to do that. Knowing how to correct mistakes is simply part of the principle.

And, for some of us, not knowing how to use calculus does not mean we can not use addition to make our lives easier. Not having a deeper understanding of the principles does not keep us from experiencing the benefits of what we do know.

Airplanes are usually off course more than they are on course. Pilots do not waste time feeling upset about being off course. They simply use the principles of navigation to keep getting back on course.

Recently I noticed thoughts which produced feelings of inadequacy. I found myself wondering, "Will these people like me? Why would they want to spend any time with me?"

In the past I would have taken those thoughts seriouly and either withdrawn and pretended I didn't care or tried to show off in some way to *make* them like me. I noticed the thoughts, dismissed them, and enjoyed myself. Next time I may act on thoughts of inadequacy and not enjoy myself.

The principles let me know when I am on course (because I feel great) and when I am off course (because I do not feel great).

When I am able to dismiss the content of my think - ing, I feel grateful. When I do not drop these thoughts, I continue to feel bad.

My present level of understanding has increased the amount of time I feel great. I would be silly to believe the principles are not valid because my understanding is not yet deep enough that I never have a negative thought. It is deep enough that I do not take those thoughts as seriously as I used to, even when I am taking them seriously enough to disturb my peace at all.

When we get *caught up* in our thought systems, it is not helpful to feel guilt or blame or failure. It is helpful simply to know what is happening. Gratitude for that knowledge will be enough to help us get quiet and make room for inspiration. Then watch the magic happen.

Also, it does not help to fight our thoughts, or to try and control them. This is like fighting a whirlpool or trying to control it. If we fight and struggle when we get caught in a whirlpool, we will drown. If we relax and get very quiet, it will carry us down and spit us out the bottom so we can float to the top of the water. Understanding makes the difference. Anyone who did not know about a whirlpool would probably get very fearful and fight it. Even knowing that it is important to relax and wait for the whirlpool to spit us out the bottom, it might still be very difficult to do. It would take a lot of faith to relax in a whirlpool before having the experience of it working. However, anyone who had this information from a reliable source (someone who has had the experience) would be very foolish indeed to fight the whirlpool.

Fighting thoughts that make you unhappy is not a life and death matter. It is just a matter of happiness or unhappiness. If you want happiness, it might take faith to follow suggestions from others who understand the principles that lead to happiness. Once you experience results for yourself, you won't need to rely on the wisdom of anyone else. You will have access to your own wisdom and inspiration.

You may still be *struggling* with these ideas. It does not matter that it is impossible to *understand* the principles from your thought system. The fact that you have read this far indicates that your common sense is also *hearing,* in spite of your thoughts.

Understanding will come from your hidden wisdom when you least expect it. Not expecting it means you have quit thinking about it (quit struggling) and cleared your channel so that your common sense and wisdom can get through.

Confusion can be a good sign of progress. Confusion can mean your thought system is being scrambled. This is a good time to drop thought and stop trying to figure it out, leaving room for inspiration.

QUIET

Quiet is not necessarily an absence of action. It is an absence of negative thoughts running wild in our thought system because they are being taken seriously. True quiet is not something to do. It is a feeling.

Before *understanding,* it makes sense to get quiet (in the sense of something to do) because slowing down can make it easier to listen for a feeling and to be more open to insight. With *understanding,* quiet is natural.

Quiet is the feeling we have when we dismiss negative thoughts. If negative thoughts were inspiring frenetic activity *to prove something,* then that activity will also be dismissed, and we will *feel* and *be* more quiet.

Being quiet does not mean sacrificing productivity. We will simply be more selective in what we want to produce. We will also be much more efficient when negative thoughts are not interfering and keeping us blind to the obvious.

Quiet is the humility we feel in the absence of negative thoughts and beliefs. In this quiet and humble state of mind, our clear channel is open.

True quiet is total humility.

SO WHAT? BIG DEAL! WHO SAYS?

How many people live their lives making a big deal out of crazy thinking, whether it comes from their own thought system or the thought systems of others?

Understanding the principles helps us see the humor in making such a big deal out of silly thoughts. *Understanding* helps us have confidence in our own common sense and wisdom and question the wisdom of what others say.

The principles explain *so what?*

1. Understanding levels of consciousness will make it natural to stop taking low moods and negative thinking seriously so good feelings will surface.
2. Understanding separate realities will make it natural to feel compassion or interest rather than judgment.

3. Understanding that thinking is a function makes it natural to dismiss negative thoughts so that inspiration from our inherent common sense and wisdom is available.
4. Using our feelings as a compass lets us know when we have momentarily forgotten our understanding.

SUGGESTIONS

It doesn't matter if you follow any of the suggestions. The only purpose for the suggestions is to help you see the principles behind them.

If you don't **see** the wisdom behind the suggestions, they will only be seen as more *rules* and *shoulds* and will create more insecurity, rebellion, argument, or some other kind of dissatisfaction.

If you don't **see** it, forget about it. Don't *think* about it. Just keep *listening* from your heart. Insight will creep up on you when you least expect it.

Suggestions about what *to do* will be meaningful only if you **see** the wisdom behind the suggestion for yourself. If you **see** the wisdom, the suggestions will trigger your own insight and inspiration. You will feel something like, "Of course! That makes sense."

Insight means you have captured the feeling rather than the words. That feeling may then lead you to follow the suggestion or to do something much different. You are well on your way. No one knows how to solve your problems better than you do when you are following your wisdom, common sense, and inspiration. The whole point of this book is to help you know that.

A good feeling will lead you in what to do for positive results. Go in the direction of good feelings, and what to do will be obvious.

THOUGHT

I'm thinking
*   thoughts from long ago.*
I'm thinking
*   tomorrow, what may be so.*
I forget I'm thinking.
It's not thought
*   this is real.*
I forget that what I think
*   determines how I feel.*

I'm missing
life before my eyes.
I'm missing
*   beauty*
*   in favor of lies.*

What I see is me.
I thought it was you.
The observed exists only
*   in the eyes of the observer's view.*
The pot calls the kettle black
*   for only blackness sees black.*

I realize I'm thinking.
*   I laugh*
*   and life is beautiful.*

Chapter 8

WHAT THOUGHTS ARE YOU WILLING TO GIVE UP YOUR HAPPINESS FOR?

One day I put a nice oak table in the garage for storage. Other family members started putting their junk (treasures to them) on the table. I complained and nagged, "Don't put your things on the oak table or it will get scratched."

No one listened. They continued to put everything on it from tools and bicycle parts, to a worn out car battery.

Finally, I went into the garage and cleaned off all the junk so I could cover it with something to protect it. Sure enough, it was scratched and gouged.

I was angry! Fortunately I had some errands to do so no one was around to listen to me. I was driving around, totally lost in my negative thoughts -- taking them very seriously.

My feelings let me know that my anger was only hurting me, making me feel upset and miserable. As soon as I became aware of what I was doing to myself with my thoughts, my mood changed. I had to laugh as I began to see things differently.

Common sense has a wonderful sense of humor. I realized it was not my family who had been irresponsible for putting things on the table. I had been irresponsible by not putting something on it to protect it in the first place.

Then inspiration let me see that I was living my life for scratches in an oak table when there were so many other, much nicer possibilities. It was a beautiful day, and I had been missing it. I had so many things to be grateful for, and I was taking them all for granted. A question came from wisdom, **"What thoughts are you willing to give up your happiness for?"**

55

Everyone who hears this story thinks it is really funny that I didn't see the obvious from the very beginning and have enough sense to cover the table in the first place. This is the point. Craziness is usually obvious to anyone who is not *caught up* in it. When we are caught up in a certain way of interpreting the world, it seems like the only possible reality.

When we are angry -- that is all we *see*. We have created a world full of bitterness.

When we are loving, we create a world of love, compassion, understanding, forgiveness, beauty, gratitude, satisfaction, and peace of mind.

Happiness and beauty are always right in front of our eyes, yet we often cover up our natural good feelings with negative thoughts. Negative thoughts create negative emotions which shut out the beauty of life. We then miss so much. **What we think is what we get.**

WHICH PRINCIPLE IS THE MOST IMPORTANT?

The principles are all interrelated. It doesn't matter which comes first. Sometimes we will see beauty everywhere because we are in a *good mood or high level of consciousness.*

Other times when we are *caught up in negative thinking, remembering that thoughts are just thoughts,* will raise our level of consciousness so that we **see** things differently.

Sometimes, when we are invested in thinking we are *right* about something, remembering the *fact of separate realities*, may create humility. We will then **see** all realities as interesting rather than right or wrong.

Another time, we may use our *feelings as a compass* to let us know we are off track. That alone may raise our mood level, or we may know we need to **get quiet until understanding comes from inspiration.**

HOW LONG DOES IT TAKE FOR UNDERSTANDING TO COME?

Sometimes in an instant; sometimes longer.
Syd Banks, philosopher and author of *Second Chance*,* received instant *understanding* from one statement, which he *heard*. He was walking along the beach with a friend who said to him, "You are not insecure, you just think you are." Syd *heard* that statement so deeply that he could not sleep for three days and three nights because he was experiencing the beauty of life so profoundly for the first time. His *understanding* changed his life as he **saw** the truth in that instant.

Syd asked his friend if he realized what he had just said. He said, "Of course I do." But he didn't. His friend continued to get *caught* up in his thoughts and to take them seriously, instead of *realizing* (as he had told Syd) he just *thought* they were serious.

This story could give the impression that *understanding* is an all or nothing event -- which it can be. It can also be a gradual process of levels of understanding. For many of us, understanding deepens as we keep listening from our common sense, wisdom, and inspiration.

Understanding is actually moment-to-moment. We may have understanding at one moment, and cover it up with thoughts the next moment. Or we may have understanding in certain areas and lack understanding in others. Our feelings will let us know. When we are experiencing positivity, we are coming from *understanding*. When we are experiencing negativity, we are coming from a lack of understanding. As our understanding deepens, we find more and more joy and peace of mind in life.

When I first heard these principles, my common sense *knew* they were true. However, my thought system drove me crazy for a year and a half with, "Yes, buts," and, "How abouts," and, "What ifs." My common sense kept *leading me back* to hear more, even though my old thought system kept getting in the way of understanding.

Second Chance by Syd Banks

Understanding was not instantaneous for me. My questions gradually changed from, "Yes, buts, how abouts, and, what ifs," to, "Tell me more."

It is amazing how often we can see what is causing our negative feelings and instantly laugh. At other times thoughts we have from our thought system may seem so real that we would bet our last dollar on them. As our understanding increases, we experience more of the former, and less of the latter.

The learning never ends. Once we get pointed in this direction, life just keeps getting nicer and nicer. Life keeps improving even when there is complete satisfaction with the way things are.

COMPASS CHART

The following chart is a graphic representation of the states of mind we experience when thinking from our clear channel, and the states we experience when thinking from our programed thought system.

CLEAR CHANNEL *High level consciousness*	THOUGHT SYSTEM *Low level consciousness*
Security	Insecurity
Love	Judgment
Happiness	Coping
Compassion	Expectations
Satisfaction	Dissatisfaction
Understanding	Assumptions
Insight	Stress
Realization	Rules (shoulds/shouldn'ts)
Forgiveness	Right vs. wrong
Gratitude	Blame
Sense of Humor	Anger
Common Sense	Interpretations
Wisdom	Anxiety
Inspiration	Proving ego
Peace of Mind	Inadequacy
The beauty of now	Past or future oriented
Natural positive feelings	Positive thinking

We all go in and out of these states of mind every day, depending on what thoughts we are thinking. Remembering that we think makes it natural to change our thoughts, and thus our mental state. Mental illness or mental health is simply a moment-to-moment state of mind. Mental illness or unhappiness are states that occur when we forget that thinking is a function.

Thoughts based on any of the concepts in the column on the right are likely to decrease happiness. Are any of them worth giving up our happiness for?

Try adding other words to the columns. A word like responsibility feels like duty or compulsiveness when added to the thought system column. Responsibility feels natural and easy when added to the clear channel column. Notice how different sex feels in either column; or charity, strength, giving, discipline, teaching, control, or any other concept you can think of.

Also notice what happens when you take some of the words from the clear channel column and add them to the thought system column. Love and forgiveness do not have the same feeling when shifted to the thought system column.

POSITIVE THINKING -- AN ERRONEOUS CONCEPT

Did you wonder why positive thinking was in the column on the right? The control we have over our ability to think is not the same as positive thinking as it is commonly taught today. Positive thinkers forget that they have the ability to think. They assume that thoughts *happen* to them, and that through positive thinking they can control which thoughts happen or can change the ones that have already happened to them. So, the battle begins.

When we are enjoying a beautiful sunset or feeling love, wouldn't it be ridiculous to stop and say, "I'd better start thinking positive about this." Even to have the thought of positive thinking means we are having negative thoughts which we think we *should* change.

There are no *shoulds* involved when we understand the principles. There are just natural positive feelings and obvious things to do to experience positive results in our lives and relationships. The battleground is eliminated. If we are experiencing a battle in our minds, we are in our thought systems, not our common sense and wisdom.

Positive thinking is also conditional. "I will be happy if I have positive thoughts," or "I'm a success when I think positive, and a failure when I don't." It is true that we will be happy if we have positive thoughts, but when positive thoughts are coming from our common sense and wisdom, they are natural and do not take effort.

Have you ever wanted to think positively and felt like a failure because you couldn't do it? Perhaps what you are learning now will help you understand why it *seems to work* sometimes and not others.

When you see things positively it is not because of positive thinking. It is because you *see* positively. Even if you saw something negatively a few moments ago, it takes insight from within to *see* it differently.

Eight-year-old Annie experienced this after a fight with her brother. She went into her room and tried to forget about it by thinking about things she enjoys. First she thought about baseball. That didn't work. She just thought about hitting her brother with a baseball bat. She tried thinking about socker, but felt like kicking her brother instead of the ball.

Annie realized that any kind of thinking didn't help. She quit thinking and started looking out the window. She watched the birds, and enjoyed looking at the trees and flowers. She became engrossed in *now* instead of thinking positively or negatively about the past. It was not long before Annie felt good again. She apologized to her brother and spent the rest of the afternoon playing with him.

Positive thinking comes from our programed thought systems and takes effort. Thinking that is truly positive is the *natural* expression of beautiful feelings which come through our clear channel in all the positive forms such as inspiration, gratitude, and unconditional love.

THE BRAIN AS A COMPUTER

The brain is like a perfect computer. However, like a computer, it is only as useful as the software put into it and the operator's ability to use it.

Using our distorted thought system is like using the old, outdated software full of bugs. It is also like trying to use a computer without ever reading the instructions or understanding the basic principles of how a computer works. Both produce unsatisfactory results.

You are now *reading the instructions* to gain an understanding of the principles that produce beautiful results in life.

Many people do not realize their thoughts are not them, just as software is not the computer. I have seen several different versions of cartoons where someone is smashing a computer with a large object because *it won't work* properly.

When we take our negative thoughts seriously, we are using as much sense as people in the cartoons who do not know that the problem is their lack of understanding or bugs in the software, not the computer.

Computer buffs also know what happens when they try to feed new information into a software program that is not designed to understand the new information. The computer beeps and flashes the words *syntax error* on the screen. Even though the new information could improve the capabilities of the software program tremendously, it simply cannot accept it.

Our brain often does the same thing with new information that could be very useful to us. When we try to filter this information through our thought system, it *beeps* a lot and says, *wrong*.

Fortunately, we have something a computer does not have -- common sense and wisdom to let us know what new information is useful to improve our lives and relationships, and what information is not useful. However, we don't have access to the wisdom until we dismiss the thought system.

*Dismissing thoughts does not leave a void. It clears the channel so thinking can be **naturally** used to express common sense, wisdom, and inspiration.*

What thought system (software) are you willing to give up your happiness for?

USING OUR CLEAR CHANNEL, RATHER THAN OUR THOUGHT SYSTEM

When we are in higher levels of consciousness our thoughts will be used to express good feelings. In lower levels of consciousness we use our thought system against ourselves.

Not long ago, I was using my thought system to make myself miserable. I was very upset because I thought a friend was being very inconsiderate.

My feelings let me know what I was doing. My stomach was churning and I couldn't sleep. It became clear to me that I was giving up my happiness for some negative thoughts.

My awareness was followed by a message from my common sense, "Which is worse, inconsiderateness or judgmentalness?" I had to laugh at my self-righteousness. Then I could see that it was not even a matter of better or worse. Inconsiderateness and judgmentalness are both simply forms of thought-provoked insecurity.

Perspective and compassion quickly followed as I remembered many of the times I have been inconsiderate -- either because I did not know better, or because I believed I was justified. I also realized that just because I thought she was being inconsiderate did not mean she was. All it meant was that she was not living up to some rules and beliefs I had created from my programed thought system. I laughed at those thoughts also, and could then feel love and gratitude for my friend and for myself.

When happiness is more important to you than anything else, you will be happy, because there will not be any thoughts you will be willing to give up your happiness for.

there are strings attached -- expectations such as, "If I am nice, then things should turn out my way."

The world looks and feels so different when we get beyond our thought system. When we are *nice* because it feels like the natural thing to do we will experience satisfaction and contentment. There are no strings attached. There is true joy in the doing.

When I was locked into my thought system, I did not like going to my children's special events such as soccer and little league games. I would go begrudgingly because I thought, "This is what *good* mothers do."

I did not enjoy these events very much and would take a book to read so I would not get too bored. I *thought* there were at least twelve other things I *should* be doing.

Recently I went to three bike races with Mark. We started at 9:00 a.m. and finished at 7:00 p.m. I did not take a book, and I did not think about twelve other things I should be doing. I had a good time and was interested in what was going on. I asked many questions and started using bike racing lingo. Mark was delighted and said, "You are starting to sound like David's dad."

This day at the races was not something I thought I should do. It was what I *felt like* doing as a natural result of feeling content with life and what it has to offer. I had a wonderful time with Mark.

All those twelve other things I once *thought* I needed to do were *busy work* attempts to prove my self-worth. I was on a *rat race* of *doing*. The twelve things I thought I should do *to prove something* never proved anything, and I would try twelve more. I was missing the enjoyment of my children in favor of the illusion of proving my self-importance, which never brought any lasting satisfaction. I had turned my back away from lasting treasures to follow the false illusions of silly thoughts.

Sometimes we might feel *inspired* to do something nice. Then our thoughts sneak in and turn it into a *should*. We will know this has happened when our feelings change from happiness to stress and anxiety or resentment.

A FAIRY TALE

Once upon a time there were two fairy princesses, Princess Dew and Princess Bee.

Princess Dew was very busy running around *doing* things for other people -- trying to make them happy. Some people loved what Princess Dew did for them. The only problem was, it didn't make them happy. They just wanted more. Princess Dew tried very hard to do more for them, hoping that someday they would be happy.

Other people did not like what she did for them *for their own good.* They wished she would stop interfering.

Princess Dew became worn out, bitter, and frustrated because people did not appreciate all she did for them. She was very unhappy. No one wanted to be around her.

Princess Bee was also very busy -- being happy. She enjoyed everything -- rainbows and clouds, rainy days and sunny days. She especially enjoyed people. She loved watching them *be.* It never occurred to her to interfere in their *being.* People loved being around her. They became very happy.

SERVICE

The fairy tale of Princess Bee and Princess Dew is not meant to imply that we should not do things for others. A happy state of mind will probably inspire us to be of service to others in any way we can. However, what we do will not come from shoulds, it will not be conditional, and it will not have ulterior motives. Service will be for the joy of the moment.

On the other hand taking care of ourselves is not selfish. The greatest thing we can **do** for ourselves and our relationships is to **be happy.**

SELFISHNESS

It is very popular to have strong negative opinions about selfishness. It is true that selfishness which comes from the thought system looks and feels like the popular beliefs about it. However, selfishness which comes from a

66

happy state of mind and wisdom does not look or feel like traditional selfishness.

I know this sounds like double talk until you **see** the difference, which is in the feeling. Selfishness from the thought system is based on ego, self-importance, resentment, rebellion, or total disregard for others.

Selfishness from a clear channel is based on feelings of love and the joy of living. With these feelings, we will want to do whatever wisdom leads us to do to enjoy life.

Because of our old *beliefs* about selfishness, we could let our thought system take over and tell us that what we want to do is *selfish*. If we stick to following the feeling, we will know the difference -- no matter what anyone else thinks.

One day Mary felt like going for a nice, long walk. She received a message from her thought system, "You should not go for a walk when you have so many other things to do, like shopping and cleaning the house." She went for a walk anyway and enjoyed the beautiful day. Her family came home to a happy wife and mother. They enjoyed being around her and felt her love.

Martha also wanted to go for a walk. However, she listened to the *shoulds* from her thought system. She felt depressed and did not get much cleaning done. Her family came home to an unhappy wife and mother.

If you are asking, "How will anything ever get done if we always do what we want instead of doing what really needs to be done?" you have missed the point. The next day Martha went for a walk, but still felt depressed. Mary stayed home and cleaned house, and still felt happy.

From a happy feeling, Mary is able to know what is important for her own well being and that of her family. From an unhappy feeling, Martha will not feel satisfied no matter what she does. Martha has trouble getting her children to do their chores. Mary gets all kinds of inspiration for things to do to win the cooperation of her children. When Mary cleans house, it is because she enjoys a clean house. She is not compulsive. When Martha cleans house she is trying to prove that she is a *good* wife and mother.

When we enjoy a nice life, we will be creating peace of mind in ourselves, in our home, and in the world.

Happiness and peace of mind are contagious.

INTELLIGENCE

Joe commented to Zeke, "I'd rather be smart and miserable than a happy fool."

Wise old Zeke asked, "Is that smart?"

Some people have the opinion that it is a sign of intelligence to find fault and ugliness in the world. They call it *being realistic*. They think anyone who can't see the negativity they see is being a blind fool. Of course, these people are not happy when they are being negative.

I prefer a definition of intelligence that includes the wisdom to be happy, no matter what other people think.

Edith Bunker is often a good example. No matter what Archie does, she sees past his behavior and just loves him.

Many people are critical of Edith, "Doesn't she have enough sense to feel insulted when Archie calls her 'Dingbat?'"

Actually, Edith has enough of a childlike quality and innocence not to take it personally.

"Why doesn't she divorce that chauvinistic pig? She would be much happier without him!"

Divorce doesn't even occur to Edith. How could she be happier? Edith is usually happy.

I am not advocating that we all act like Edith Bunker. (After all, she is only the illusion of script writers.) The point is, that you will see examples of the principles on television, in literature, and in the way you and others live once you understand them.

Edith Bunker can also be a good example of not seeing things with perspective and common sense. Her happiness often depends on others.

PATIENCE

"I just lost my patience," claimed Helen.

"If only I could be more patient," sighed Henry.

And so the struggle goes when people have the opinion that patience is a matter of self-control, or a quality that must be developed. Patience is natural when we are experiencing life through our clear thought channel and feel peace of mind and contentment.

Impatience is a creation from thoughts of dissatisfaction, expectation, or judgment. Dismiss those thoughts and you have patience. It is impossible to feel impatient and satisfied at the same time.

You may ask, "How can I possibly be patient when someone is doing something I know they should not be doing?"

Turning the other cheek always seemed terribly wimpy to me. It makes sense now. When we *see* the innocence in what others do from a lack of understanding, it doesn't make sense to lash out at them, nor to lose our own peace of mind in reaction to their insecurity. It makes sense to create a loving, forgiving atmosphere where they can best gain understanding or to know when they are not ready to learn.

FORGIVENESS

Anyone who says, "I will forgive, but I won't forget." does not *understand* forgiveness. Forgiveness *is* forgetting. Dismissing negative thought and forgiveness are synonymous.

People who have the popular opinion that forgiveness is something you have to *work at* or *try to do*, are deeply engrossed in ego and judgment. It is a superiority trip to think, "Well, I know you did something *wrong*, but I will be *big* enough to *forgive* you." Or, "You did a despicable thing, and you don't deserve forgiveness."

Lack of forgiveness comes from self-righteous judgment and harms the unforgiving more than the unforgiven.

It is impossible to be happy while holding on to (rather than dismissing) judgments.

Forgiveness is natural from a level of consciousness that includes understanding, compassion, love, humor, gratitude, and peace of mind. Forgiveness is not even an issue when we have these feelings.

When we *see* with *understanding,* there is nothing to forgive.

69

CIRCUMSTANCES

Contrary to popular opinion, circumstances have nothing to do with happiness.

How often have you heard, "I'll be happy when I finish school. I'll be happy when I'm married. I'll be happy when I'm single. I'll be happy when I have more money. I'll be happy when I have children. I'll be happy when I don't have children. I'll be happy when *you* do what I want you to do."

If you are not happy before you get what you want, you won't be happy after you get it.

Happiness is a state of mind. If you are not happy before you get married, you won't be happy after you get married. If you are not happy before you have children, you won't be happy after you have children. If you are not happy with your children, you won't be happy after they are gone. If you are not happy married, you won't be happy single -- at least not for long. People who think they are happy when they first get what they want find it doesn't last long. When things settle down they feel that old, nagging insecurity and dissatisfaction. Or, they get trapped back in their feelings of unhappiness the first time things don't go the way they think they should.

I have a friend who was convinced that he would be happy when he had $100,000 in the bank. It took him thirty years of hard work, but he finally achieved his goal. He was extremely happy for about one month before he felt dissatisfied again. He was sure the answer must be $200,000. It only took ten more years to achieve that goal. Of course, his happiness did not last. He is now convinced that one million dollars will do it.

Happiness is a state of mind which allows us to **see** things differently. During a happy state of mind we **see** life with gratitude and perspective. From a happy state of mind, circumstances look much different than they do when seen through the filter of our thought system. When we are in a happy state of mind, what *to do* comes from inspiration. What to do seems obvious, and will be loving. There are no strings attached because we realize that our happiness has nothing to do with external circumstances.

Happiness is a state of mind that comes from within.

You may be wondering, "But what about things that are beyond my control, like sickness or negative things other people do?" When we have peace of mind and contentment we see **what is** without judgment like the wise man in the following story.

A HORSE STORY

Many years ago a wise man lived in an old mountain village. One day a beautiful, wild stallion ran into his corral. When the villagers heard the news they came to his farm and marveled, "What a wonderful thing! You are so lucky!"

The wise man replied, "Maybe so, maybe not."

A few days later the stallion broke the corral fence and ran away. When the villagers heard the news they came to his farm and said, "What a terrible thing! What bad luck!"

The wise man replied, "Maybe so, maybe not."

The next day the stallion returned bringing a whole herd of mares. When the villagers heard the news they came and exclaimed, "Now you are the richest man in the village, and surely the luckiest!"

The wise man replied, "Maybe so, maybe not."

The wise man's son tried to break one of the mares. He was thrown and broke his leg. When the villagers heard the news they came and sympathized, "What a tragedy! Who will help you now with the harvest? This is such an unlucky thing to happen!"

The wise man replied, "Maybe so, maybe not."

The next day the Cossacks came to get all the young men of the village to fight their wars. They did not take the wise man's son because of his broken leg.

SEEING *WHAT IS* WITHOUT JUDGMENT

You may ask, "But what if I'm not in a high enough state of mind to see things without judgment. What if I do have negative thoughts and feelings about external circumstances?"

When we are confronted with circumstances we can't seem to *understand* and we add negative thoughts to them, we have two things we don't like -- the circumstances and our thoughts about them. Our negative thoughts are usually much worse than the circumstances. It is our thoughts that produce our feelings.

We don't see the beauty of life and experience feelings of joy and gratitude when we waste time and energy on judgments. Judgments fill us with toxic feelings.

A good example is the story of two men who lost their fortunes. One had extremely negative thoughts about his circumstances and jumped off a building. The other man saw it as an opportunity to have the adventure of starting over again in something new.

By the way, the man who jumped off the building was not a happy person even when he had his fortune. The man who saw the opportunity had been enjoying life during all his varied circumstances.

WHO ME? I THOUGHT IT WAS *YOU*, *IT*, *THEM*

Your world is created by how you see it. How you see it is directly related to the filters in your thought system, or your lack of filters so you can see the world freshly from your clear channel.

Do I hear an argument? "I can understand how that applies to most circumstances, but not others."

It is interesting how often people try to find the most extreme cases where they think a principle *might* not be true, in order to invalidate it, instead of simply applying the principle to situations in their own lives, where they *know* it is true.

I have found that as I experience the principles in areas where I do not doubt, my understanding deepens. I then doubt less and see the principles in areas I have formerly been unable to understand.

This is a direction that never ends. *Understanding* keeps deepening, and life keeps getting more beautiful. Actually life is always beautiful. We either see it or we don't.

Chapter 10

DETOURS

There are many detours which keep us from the treasures of happiness and peace of mind.

INSECURITY

Insecurity is just another thought. There is really no such thing. **Try to feel insecure without thinking you are insecure.** It is impossible.

Many therapists claim they can help others, even when they believe in their own insecurities. They claim, "At least I know how to cope with my insecurities. I know how to handle them."

These therapists are not much better off than their clients because they still see insecurity as real, rather than a thought. Coping may be better than not coping, but it falls far short of happiness and peace of mind.

Even though insecurity is just another thought, it becomes very powerful when taken seriously. The illusion of insecurity is the cause of all negativity.

Thought-provoked insecurity may take many forms, such as agressiveness, drug abuse, shyness, the need to prove one's worth through power or achievements, wars, self-righteousness, or feelings of inadequacy. Every negative act is based on thoughts which produce the illusion of insecurity.

Like other illusions, insecurity loses its power once we know what it is. *Understanding* inspires love and compassion for ourselves and others, who may not know that their negative behavior is based on the illusion of insecurity.

73

JUDGMENTS

There is a form of judgment that is very helpful. If we see a truck speeding toward us, we will probably make the judgment that it would be a good idea to get out of the way. To add the *judgment* that every truck is dangerous and stuff our thought systems with a fear of trucks would be a useless burden.

Many excuse their judgments of others by calling it *righteous judgment*. Righteous judgment is very rare. Righteous judgment would not leave any negative feelings in its wake. It would be based on feelings of love and understanding. The results of righteous judgment would be positive.

"I'm telling you this for your own good," is not an example of righteous judgment. This is an example taking your own separate reality seriously and thinking it is the *right* reality.

Self-righteous judgment of others is not helpful. It leaves negative feelings. Negative feelings are the compass which let us know that we are caught up in our thought system. As soon as we become aware of our thought system, it loses power.

When we dismiss judgment for the thought that it is, we rise to a higher level of consciousness where judgments are replaced with love, compassion, and inspiration about what to do.

Debra was having negative feelings about her friend Georgia. Georgia was living her life in ways that *looked* very negative to Debra. Debra did not want to be around Georgia for awhile, which could have been a reasonable solution if Debra had kept it simple and stayed away without judgment of Georgia or herself. However Debra contaminated her decision by judging herself, "If I were a bigger person, I wouldn't let her behavior bother me. I should be more loving and understanding."

Her thoughts of self-judgment kept her in a low mood which limited her perspective. From this perspective she kept judging her friend. "She is being so self-centered, self-righteous, manipulating, and self-serving. She thinks her reality is the only valid one in the world." Debra was able to find several other people who had the same judgments about Georgia, which she saw as justification for her thoughts.

Debra's stomach was in knots as she continued the vicious cycle of self-condemnation and judgment of Georgia.

Debra finally saw her judgments for the thoughts that they were. As soon as she dismissed them she was able to stay away from a situation which did not feel good to her, but she did it without judgment of herself or her friend. She realized it was true that someday her understanding might get deep enough that her friend's behavior would not bother her, but until then she would stay away, without judgment.

There is a world of difference between walking away from a situation with judgment, and walking away without judgment. Our common sense may tell us to walk away from a situation, but it will never tell us to judge it in the sense of having negative feelings against someone or something.

Being without judgment is a *state of humility and quiet.* During the *quiet* Debra's *understanding* deepened. The next time she saw Georgia, her negative feelings were gone. In her present state of understanding, she had a deeper appreciation of everything in life, including her friend Georgia. She knew that what she had seen in Georgia before was only a reflection of thoughts and *beliefs* about how things *should* be according to the reality of her ego.

STEREOTYPING

Another danger of judgment is that we often judge a person for what they do when they are in a *bad mood* and decide this is the sum total of *who they are.* We often dismiss what they do when they are in a good mood as *just an act.*

JUDGMENTS FROM OTHERS

With *understanding,* we do not pay any more attention to the judgments of others than to our own. We see that we get into enough trouble taking our own judgments seriously. Shoulds and shouldn'ts are not any more helpful from others that they are from ourselves.

This does not mean we will judge other people's thoughts. We will simply know that they are just thoughts, and then we will see them with compassion, interest, or humor.

Virginia dreaded being around her mother for long because she felt intimidated by her judgments, which she reacted to with rebellion. Her mother reacted to Virginia's rebellion with more judgments.

After learning about the principles, Virginia spent a delightful four days traveling across the country with her mother. As Virginia tells the story, "Every time my Mom would come out with what I used to call a judgment, I just saw it as her reality. Instead of rebelling and letting her know I thought what she thought was stupid, I saw it as interesting. I still didn't agree with her on everything, but I respected her right to see things differently. I also was able to respect my way of seeing things, without getting huffy about it. We had a great time. We talked and shared more than we have in my whole life."

A BREAD STORY

Once there was a little girl named Marie, who went to visit her Aunt and Uncle and learned how to make bread. Her Aunt and Uncle thought that was wonderful. They praised her and told her over and over how much they appreciated her breadmaking.

Marie went home and baked bread for her family. No one said anything about her bread. They just ate it.

Marie decided she would never make bread for her family again because they didn't appreciate it and praise her.

Then one day she discovered how much fun it was to make bread for herself. She loved getting her hands into the dough to knead it. She loved the smell of the bread baking in the oven. She especially loved eating it hot out of the oven, dripping with butter and sometimes honey. And, she loved sharing it with anyone who wanted to have some.

She realized that as long as she was living *for* or *against* someone else, she missed the bread.

76

EGO AND SELF-IMPORTANCE

The illusions of insecurity are strongly attached to the illusions of ego and proving self-importance. Ego assumes there is something to prove. The need to prove self-importance is based on the assumption that it is possible not to be important. In a sense that is true, because being important usually means *more important than someone else*, which we are not.

It is impossible to find happiness through trying to prove self-importance. The basis for the search (the belief that it is possible to be unimportant) guarantees failure. Temporary relief might be found through some kind of achievement, but it doesn't last. The insecurity is still lurking and must be constantly fed in order to exist, at the same time one is trying to prove it doesn't exist. It is exhausting even to think about it.

When you get off track into your thought system, notice how often it is over issues that challenge your thoughts and beliefs about proving your self-importance or how you think life or others should be.

The fun thing about ego is that every time we recognize it for what it is, we can't help laughing at it. Then it disappears. However, our ego loves catching us off guard so that it can sneak back.

Have you ever played hide-and-seek with your ego? It can be fun to *catch ourselves* getting involved in our ego. We have always had fun catching it in others (unless we turned it into judgment.) Now we can have fun catching ourselves.

Being concerned about the judgments of others is just another ego trip. When we are ego-involved, we can feel intimidated about what others say. When we dismiss ego, we are not affected by what others say.

SELF-CENTERING ON SELF-ESTEEM

Self-esteem is the natural well-being you feel when you stop centering on your *self*. Self-esteem is like happiness. You can't find it by looking for it. Self-esteem and happiness are inherent and natural in human beings when they dismiss the thought system which keeps them buried.

An extremely popular detour is the one of *working on* self-esteem. Since lack of self-esteem is an illusion which can not exist without thoughts from the thought system, it does not make sense to give the illusion credibility by trying to attain self-esteem. The idea that a human being could not have self-worth is a very silly thought. This thought is based on other silly thoughts about what a person must *do, be, achieve, look like, or own.* It is much easier to simply dismiss thoughts that create the illusion of lack of self-esteem.

Being *self*-centered on *self*-esteem is a detour guaranteed to lead you away from your natural self-esteem.

ANGER

We get angry when our thoughts that create ego and self-importance get very busy deciding that the world should revolve around us. We can spend a lot of time on this detour away from happiness, since the world never does revolve around us.

It doesn't take much to make me angry when my ego thoughts are in control. I get angry when people don't drive the way I want them to, and when my husband doesn't respond the way I want him to, at exactly the moment I want him to, (preferably by reading my mind about what I want.) I get angry when my family and friends don't behave the way I want them to, and always live up to my expectations. I get angry when equipment doesn't work the way I want it to, and when business people don't think I am the most important customer they have. I especially get angry when someone else gets angry at me. This is about one-tenth of my list.

When I see my anger as reality, I have different ways of expressing it. Sometimes I verbalize anger, sometimes I sulk, and, sometimes I have a silent temper tantrum against myself and get depressed.

My list of justifications as to why the world should revolve around me is much shorter. It *should* because my reality is the *right* one. Thoughts that create ego and thoughts that create self-righteousness walk through our thought system hand in hand.

78

Anger is nothing more than ego being expressed in a temper tantrum. I jokingly and fondly refer to this as SBS (spoiled brat sydrome). I was once president of the SBS Club. The Club was abolished when I learned that anger and SBS cannot exist without thought.

There is a popular opinion that if you don't get your anger out, you will store it, and it will fester. This is not true. Festering is caused when you keep taking negative thoughts seriously and keep thinking about them. When you forget about the thoughts that create negative feelings, they are not stored. You have to think about the thoughts again to re-create the bad feelings. If you think about those negative thoughts again after forgetting about them for awhile, it is not because they were stored. You were simply distracted from thinking about them for awhile, even though you still took them seriously, and then re-created them again.

Another popular belief is that there are certain things that justify anger. Not true again. Anger does not solve anything. It just makes you feel bad and keeps you from enjoying life **now.**

One therapist worked in group therapy with 60 women who had been victims of rape or incest. For many years these women talked about their anger, beat on pillows, yelled and screamed about their anger. They spent hours confirming that what had happened to them in the past was the reason they could not hold jobs, were alcoholics, and could not participate in lasting relationships.

This therapist learned about the principles. She apologized to the women in her groups, "I'm sorry, ladies, but I have been doing it all wrong. From now on we will no longer dwell on the past, but will talk about some principles which will teach you how to have happiness and peace of mind in life now."

A few women dropped out of her groups because they did not want to give up their anger. The other women soon learned to enjoy life. A two year follow-up showed that they maintained their good feelings and were successful in their jobs and relationships. Some were training to become therapists or educators so they could share what they had learned.

When we don't like what happened in the past, it doesn't make sense to keep recreating it in our thoughts, and then to multiply the unhappiness we create by adding anger.

Like all negative thoughts, anger loses its power when seen with perspective. As soon as you can laugh at anger, or at least see it for what it is, anger is gone.

THE PAST

Another popular detour is into the past. The past cannot exist unless we think about it, yet many live their whole lives on this detour.

Our brain does not store what happened in the past. The thought system stores our interpretations of what happened. It is our interpretations (thoughts) about what happened that creates our emotions.

It is impossible to store emotions. We keep recreating the same negative emotions when we keep thinking about our old interpretations.

Our interpretations are hardly ever correct. Any time we choose to interpret an event differently, our emotions and reactions will also change.

Linda had an experience in her past where it seemed to her that her father felt embarrassed to hug her. She interpreted that to mean he didn't love her, which she interpreted to mean she was not lovable. If she was not lovable to her father, that must mean she was not lovable to anyone. So she started living her life feeling insecure because of her thought that she was unlovable.

Linda constantly tried to prove she was lovable, but because her behavior was based on insecurity, she acted demanding and unlovable. Besides, she really believed she was not lovable, so she would not have accepted any proof that she was lovable anyway.

She would constantly ask her husband if he really loved her. He was very patient and kept reassuring her that he did. Linda either didn't believe him, or would lose respect for him for loving such an unlovable person. This all became hilarious to her once she dismissed her interpretations and her thoughts of insecurity and saw the ridiculousness of the whole comedy.

When stuck in any of these illusions of the past, we miss life, yet many people believe these illusions are real -- that they are life. All this insanity is eliminated through *understanding* thought.

When we understand that the past cannot exist unless we think about it and is only our interpretations of what happened anyway, it becomes difficult to take our thoughts about the past seriously.

Also, when we see the innocence of anything anyone else did in the past, knowing that they did the best they could from their present level of understanding, we will feel differently about them.

Paula often complained about all the terrible things her mother had done and said to her in the past. A therapist asked her, "Do you think your mother stayed up late at night plotting how she could make your life miserable?"

With reluctance Paula admitted, "No."

A week later Paula shared that she had gained a great deal of insight. It became clear to her that her mother really did love her and did the best she could based on all the insecurities she felt in life.

Paula added that she now was able to see how she was repeating many of the *mistakes* she had been complaining about with her own son and gave the following example, "I punish him when he makes mistakes even though I hated it when my mother did that. I can see now that she probably did it for the same reasons I do. I'm afraid that if I don't punish him he won't learn to do better, and I want him to do better because I love him. But when I was a child I can remember wishing my Mother would understand how I felt and teach me with love instead of punishment."

Paula was able to forgive her mother and herself when she understood that the *mistakes* they both had made were simply the results of getting sidetracked from love and enjoyment of their children into thoughts that produced fear and insecurity.

DECISIONS

Contrary to popular behavior, it is not helpful to *figure things out* or make decisions when feeling stress. This only keeps us deeply enmeshed in our thought system.

It is as ineffective as keeping our foot on the gas pedal to get out of a ditch, even though the spinning wheel digs deeper and deeper into the sand.

If you have any doubts about what to do, or want to do something because of negative feelings such as anger; let that be your clue that you are *lost in your thought system.*

Decisions from our common sense and wisdom are always positive and produce good results. We know when decisions are inspiration from our common sense and wisdom, and there is no doubt about appropriateness. They don't even feel like *decisions*

Actually, the concept of decision-making changes with *understanding.* The familiar concept of decision-making implies choice or effort. With *understanding* decisions feel more like obvious, common sense things to do than like choice or effort.

A decision may make sense in one situation. However, if we make a rule out of it, we will lose touch with our common sense and wisdom. No matter how similar the situation, it may call for a completely different decision at another time. Only our common sense knows.

One day I realized I had made a rule out of not spreading my low moods around. In other words, I had decided I *should* never talk about it. Now I can see that not talking about it is a possibility that makes sense most of the time. However, one day I felt like talking with a good friend about a situation which I knew I was seeing through my judgmental glasses. My *shoulds* got very busy in my thought system. "I should not be spreading this around. I should be able to dismiss it and go to a higher level of consciousness." Then my ego joined in, "He is going to think I don't know anything since I can't stay in a high level of consciousness." I talked about it anyway, and while I was listening to myself and to him, I gained insights that made it easy and natural to dismiss my judgments and see with perspective again.

I was again reminded that the principles are not a basis for judgment regarding shoulds or shouldn'ts, but simply give us an understanding of what happens when we do what we do. Even a limited understanding of the principles keeps us pointed in the right direction so that our understanding keeps getting deeper. The deeper the understanding, the easier it gets.

Let good feelings from you common sense and wisdom be your only guide.

PART THREE

JOY IN RELATIONSHIPS

Chapter 11

MARRIAGE

The principles show us where all problems in a marriage originate.

1. Trying to change realities -- fighting over who is right instead of respecting differences and finding them interesting.
2. Getting caught up in negative thoughts -- judgments, interpretations, the past, proving ego and self-importance, spoiled bratness, and other forms of thought produced insecurity, which happens when we focus on the content of our thoughts instead of realizing the fact of thinking as a function.
3. Not dismissing negative thoughts during low moods or low levels of consciousness, but instead, trying to discuss them, figure them out, or solve them.
4. Sharing negative feelings that come from the insecurity of our thought systems instead of sharing only the positive feelings that come from wisdom and inspiration.

SEPARATE REALITIES RELATING TO MARRIAGE

Amy and Sean had arguments every day. No matter what the subject, the theme was always the same.

Amy, "You have to be blind as a bat not to see things my way!"

Sean, "If you had any brains at all, you would know that my way is right!"

What good are eyes and brains without understanding and wisdom? Amy and Sean are both stuck in the illusions of their separate realities.

Have you had the experience of trying to convince your partner that your point of view is the right one, and felt like you were talking to a wall? Actually talking to a wall can be easier because a wall does not have it's own point of view. You don't have any expectations from a wall. You would feel pretty silly trying to convince a wall that your interpretation of *how things are* is the *right* interpretation.

It is even less productive to try convincing your spouse, who already *knows* how things *are,* and would like to convince you. Your partner is usually seeing his or her reality with as much perspective as you are seeing yours. Zero.

Jeanette strongly believed her children needed lots of rules and guidance. Duane believed he should sacrifice anything that was important to him in order to cater to their whims.

Duane thought Jeanette was a tyrant. Jeanette thought Duane was a wimp. Both were so lost in their separate realities and thought systems that they could not **see** clearly or with perspective. All the children needed was love and common sense. Sometimes common sense might take the form of guidance, and sometimes it might take the form of doing things with them or for them. In either case, guidance or doing things for them will be entirely different when based on good feelings and inspiration than when it is based on insecurity in the form of self-righteousness, defensiveness, or judgment.

When we take our reality seriously, it becomes a very interesting frame of reference -- or distorted pair of glasses. We don't realize how those glasses distort and filter everything in our world. When we dismiss our judgments and expectations, we **see** a very different and interesting person in front of us.

Dorene and Charles were experiencing marital difficulty because they were deeply enmeshed in their separate realities. Their distorted frames of reference prevented them from seeing anything with common sense and wisdom.

Dorene complained about being third or fourth priority in Charles' life. This thought quickly became a belief from which she was able to generate hurt feelings. She continued to complicate matters by thinking she needed to cover her hurt feelings with anger. She gained a false sense of security by feeling angry instead of hurt. She expressed her anger by blaming and attacking Charles for not putting her first.

Charles took her attacks seriously and generated feelings of inadequacy and defensiveness which he expressed by acting disdainful toward Dorene. Charles' frame of reference included a belief that women were unfair and unreasonable anyway.

Neither were aware that they were not seeing each other clearly in the present. They were seeing each other and circumstances through distorted beliefs from the past which they had programed into their thought systems.

Somewhere in Dorene's past she had an experience which she interpreted to mean that she was not important. She turned this interpretation into a belief which distorted every experience she had from then on. Without being aware of what she was doing, she spent her life looking for evidence to support her belief that she was not important. She was so intent on this task that she missed any evidence that might change her belief.

This was obvious when she told the story of how she and Charles met and got married. Charles was dating Adele. He quit seeing Adele and soon asked Dorene to marry him. Dorene did not see this as evidence that she was important to Charles. What she did notice was Adele's name on the wedding invitation list. She saw this as evidence that Adele was more important to him than she was. Explanations from Charles that he still liked Adele as a *friend* fell on deaf ears.

You and I can have enough perspective (because we are not too close) to see the humor in their silly thinking. Dorene and Charles were not laughing. When anyone takes the filters from their thought system seriously, it is impossible to see the situation with perspective.

Charles had an experience in his past which he interpreted to mean that women were unfair and unreasonable. He adopted this as such a strong belief that he did not notice how he *set women up* to prove he was right. He knew Dorene would probably be upset if he put Adele's name on the wedding invitation list. He didn't really care if Adele came to the wedding. He just wanted to be able to prove that he was right about how unreasonable women can be. Of course, he claimed to care. He had to justify his position.

Dorene and Charles were focused on what they were looking for through the filters of their thought systems. This did not leave much time to share good feelings.

When our attention is focused on looking for evidence to support our distorted beliefs, we miss the obvious, wonderful things going on around us. For example, suppose I told you I had hidden a red button in a beautifully decorated room and would give you $10,000 if you could find it in five minutes. You would probably find it. Then suppose I said, "Fine. I'll give you the $10,000 -- or, I'll give you $20,000 if you can describe the room to me." Do you think you could describe the room? Of course not. You would have missed everything around you because you were focused on looking for the red button.

We can always create what we are looking for. Anyone who believes they will be rejected will act in such a way that invites rejection. Or, they will see rejection even in innocent behaviors which do not mean rejection at all.

The truth is that it is impossible for anyone to reject another person. If someone says you are the biggest creep in the world, that statement actually has nothing to do with you. People who make remarks such as this are simply caught up in their own thought systems and are feeling insecure.

Dorene and Charles finally dismissed their insecurities and saw each other very differently. They stopped playing detectives, looking for evidence to support their insecurities. Charles felt like reassuring Dorene that she was important, and Dorene felt like reassuring Charles that she trusted him. Neither one really needed reassurance any more, but accepted the loving gestures. They had learned to laugh at their silly thoughts and see the beauty of life and of each other.

ACCEPTANCE

Acceptance means respecting differences, not conditional acceptance while waiting for changes to be made, nor tolerance for someone who obviously has not learned the *right way*. Acceptance is seeing that everyone has a separate reality. Through our clear channels we will *see* levels of insecurity in others with compassion. Through our thought systems we will see behavior through our filters of judgment.

Even though it is impossible to change other people's realities (only they can do that by changing their own thoughts) it is amazing how often we keep trying.

A marriage counselor suggested to Hazel that she stop trying to change her husband and accept him the way he was. Three months later Hazel complained, "But, I have accepted him for three whole months, and he hasn't changed a bit!"

What Hazel thought was acceptance was conditional. True acceptance is unconditional and allows us to **see** a different reality -- a reality full of gratitude, peace of mind, and joy as illustrated in the following poem:

ACCEPTANCE

When I want
more of you
I'm truly in love
with you.

When I want you
to be more
I'm in love
with a dream.

Wanting you to be more
makes me (and you) miserable.
Wanting more of you
fulfills my dreams.

UNDERSTANDING

When I want more
of you
I see you
in all your
specialness
uniqueness
magnificence
and
I am filled
with gratitude
wonder
joy.

You mean so much to me.

I want more of you.

THOUGHTS AND MOODS RELATED TO MARRIAGE

Mary thought Jim was not paying enough attention to her. She self-righteously shared this with her friends. They suggested that she let him know how she felt. Mary decided that was a good idea.

That night Jim sat down on the couch and started to read the newspaper. Mary sat next to him and said, "How come the newspaper is more important to you that I am?"

Jim defensively retorted, "Because the newspaper doesn't hassle me."

Mary ran to the bedroom and cried. For the rest of the evening she would not speak to Jim. The next day she told all her friends that Jim had admitted he preferred the newspaper to her, so she might as well get a divorce.

Fortunately Mary had an opportunity to learn about the principles. She dismissed the notions of insecurity from her thought system and was amazed how much her feelings about herself and Jim changed.

The next time Jim sat down to read the newspaper, she quiety sat next to him, feeling gratitude for having such a nice man for a husband. She could see past his insecure behavior because she had dismissed her own insecurities, judgments and expectations, and felt unconditional love.

Soon, Jim put down the newspaper and gruffly said, "Did you want to talk?" Mary could feel that he was still in a bad mood and replied, "No, I was just enjoying your presence."

Suspiciously, Jim continued to read the newspaper.

For several weeks, Mary continued to enjoy just being with Jim, no matter what he did. She had discovered her own inner happiness and peace of mind and was not affected by outside circumstances.

One day, Jim came into the kitchen while Mary was finishing dinner. She asked, "Did you want something?"

"No," Jim replied, "I just wanted to be with you."

We literally create our world from our thoughts and actions. *We reap what we sow.* When we put negativity out into the world, we get negativity back. However, when negativity comes back most people forget they put it out in the first place. They don't take responsibility for creating the negativity with their thoughts and subsequent actions.

On the other hand, when we put positivity out into the world, positivity comes back.

You can know you are feeling truly positive when you are feeling so grateful for *what is* that you don't expect anything back. Expecting something back is manipulative, conditional giving.

Are you still arguing that sometimes negative circumstances come to you even when you didn't do anything to create it?

Even if you do not have any personal responsibility for the creation of certain events, it is your thoughts that give you more trouble than the circumstances. Many people make lemonade out of lemons.

Sue's husband had an affair. She was so hurt by this that she wanted revenge. She went to an attorney and said, "I want to hurt him as much as he hurt me. I want to leave him with as little as possible financially, and to limit his child visitation rights as much as possible. I will make sure the kids don't even want to see him."

Sue could not see that it was her thoughts about this situation that were making her miserable. Fortunately she chose a very wise attorney who asked, "Do you really want to hurt him in the worst way possible?"

Sue replied, "Yes."

93

The attorney said, "Then go back and live with him for six months. Be the very best wife you can imagine. Be loving, compassionate, understanding, forgiving, affectionate, and have lots of fun with him. He will feel so lucky and will start loving you very much. In six months you can proceed to get a divorce. Then he will be hurt emotionally and financially."

Sue objected, "I couldn't stand to live with him for six more months."

The attorney said, "Well, then you must not really want to hurt him in the worst way possible."

Sue said, "Oh yes I do. I will do it."

Two years later the attorney saw Sue walking down a street. He asked, "What happened? I thought you were going to come back for a divorce."

Sue replied, "Are you kidding? He is the most wonderful man in the world. I wouldn't even think of leaving him."

Sue must have done such a good job acting loving that she soon forgot it was an act and just started enjoying the good feelings. Good feelings are extremely contagious. Good feelings create more good feelings in everyone who comes in contact with them.

When *understanding* changes how we **see** things, everything and everyone in our world looks different. It may seem as though others have changed, but it is our thoughts, and thus our reality, and thus our feelings that have changed. Others often respond to our feeling level. When we give love, we get love -- not necessarily because others give it back to us, but because love will emanate from within. Feeling love does not depend on anything or anyone else.

You may ask, "But, what if I just don't feel loving, and I am not willing to 'act' like Sue did?"

Whenever we feel the need to ask what to do, it is helpful not to do anything except to dismiss our thoughts, get quiet, and wait until we feel good enough to know from our own wisdom what to do.

Remember that sometimes awareness of the principles will change our mood instantly, and we will tap into common sense and wisdom. Other times we may see that focusing on the content of our thoughts is producing our negative feelings, but we won't feel totally better immediately. At those times, it is more like having the flu. We have a level of understanding that doesn't change our state of mind immediately, but it may lead us to quietly take care of ourselves until it does go away.

I realized this after an experience of being caught up in thinking my reality was much better than my husband's. In other words, I really believed he was wrong. Since it seemed so real to me, I certainly had to tell him about it. Have you ever noticed that when you think someone else is *wrong*, you feel compelled to let them know about it? Have you also noticed that you become *worse* with your judgments, criticisms, and self-righteousness, than the person you are judging. (*Worse* is just another judgment not to be taken seriously. Look for the principle.)

My tirade lasted about five minutes before my miserable feelings alerted me to see what I was doing. I immediately shut up, but I still didn't feel much better. I simply *saw* enough to get quiet and quit spreading it around.

I started thinking, "I should apologize." I didn't feel like it since I was still in a relatively low state of mind, so I just stayed quiet.

I don't remember how long it took for me to feel better, because I quit thinking about it; but the next day when I was feeling love and gratitude for my husband, we talked about what had happened. Since I was then in a very loving mood, it felt natural to apologize without feeling blame and guilt. Barry shared that he was very much aware that my silence the day before was not the same as my old sulky silences.

Another time I became upset when my husband and I missed an opportunity to go on a trip with friends because he had a hunting trip planned. I had several negative thoughts which gave me some very negative feelings. I knew I was caught up in my thought system, but I didn't get quiet. I asked Barry, "Would you like to hear my *garbage* thoughts?"

Barry replied good naturedly, "Sure. Go ahead."

I said, "Hunting is more important to you than I am."

Barry calmly said, "You know that isn't true. I had this planned way ahead. I'll be more than happy to take a trip with you anytime we can find a mutually agreeable time."

I admitted, "I know. I'm just doing my spoiled brat number where I think the world should revolve around me. I'll get over it soon."

In the past I have believed my silly thoughts about hunting being more important than I am. (Actually, so what if it is?) The important difference this time was that I took responsibility for my *garbage* thinking. Even though I felt disappointed, I couldn't take it as seriously as I did when I didn't know I was thinking from my thought system.

My awareness of acting like a spoiled brat made it impossible for those feelings to have much power. It was not long before I could **see** that I didn't need a trip to be happy. I don't even need to be more important than hunting to be happy.

Intellectual understanding does not change our feelings, but it can help us to dismiss our thoughts, or at least not take them too seriously, until we have *understanding* from an insight or realization.

Our feelings change when *understanding* comes though our clear channels rather than our thought systems.

LISTENING

Whenever we feel upset, we have stopped listening from love and have started listening from ego and a programed thought system. It is helpful to use our feeling of upsetness as a compass to let us know we are off track and start listening deeper.

True listening is forgetting about the details, *hearing* what another person is feeling, and knowing when those feelings are coming from thoughts of insecurity. We can know the difference from our own feeling level.

We are listening deeply when we feel love, compassion, or interest rather than judgment or defensiveness.

Understanding changes the experience of listening. It is impossible to experience another person's reality. As soon as we think we can, we have stopped listening and have started dealing with our own experience of what we *think* it is like for them. When we know this, it can be interesting to listen to another person's reality and learn as much as we can. This is possible only when we stop trying to add our own interpretations and listen without judgment.

When your partner is upset or caught up in thought, that is the time to *listen*, not talk. Analyzing does not help. Listening is quietly responding with love and understanding. When we are in that state of mind our inspiration will let us know exactly what to do to create positivity -- eventually, if not immediately. It might be humor. It might be time alone. It might be a loving touch. It might be a quiet walk. It might be time to rest. We will know.

HAVE FUN TOGETHER

Have you ever noticed that when you are having fun together you are not being judgmental, critical, or dissatisfied? When we want happiness and peace of mind, it makes sense to do things together that bring pleasure and enjoyment.

LIVE IN GRATITUDE

When we dismiss negative thoughts, we are left with feelings of gratitude and appreciation for all that life has to offer.

It does not make sense to live in negativity when positivity is just a dropped thought away.

When following the treasure map to happiness and peace of mind, **the natural state of marriage is to enjoy unconditional love.**

Chapter 12

MYTHS ABOUT MARRIAGE

As the following myths are presented, they may be very difficult to comprehend, because they are the opposite of what many of us have been taught all our lives.

MYTH NO. 1
LOVE IS BLIND

The opposite is true. When we are *in love* we are not blinded by judgments, expectations, and other kinds of insecurities. We see differences as interesting or with understanding and compassion. What other people might see as faults in our beloved, we find endearing, we defend, or brush off as unimportant.

Bob told Nancy he would call her at 9:30. He didn't call until 11:00. Nancy thought he was very inconsiderate and uncaring -- and told him so. Later she realized that when they first fell in love she had been very understanding and compassionate when he called later than promised. It became obvious to her that it wasn't the circumstances, but her thoughts which upset her and created her feelings.

When we look through our judgment glasses differences or circumstances are no longer seen with understanding, interest, or compassion. The judgment blinder is so powerful that it even changes what was once seen as a virtue into a fault.

Marilyn fell in love with Jordan and admired the calm way he drove a car. She felt so safe and relaxed on rides with him at the wheel. After they got married she found it often drove her crazy to ride with him because he was not more aggressive and didn't take risks to pass slow cars.

Another thing Marilyn had admired about Jordan was his quiet, easy-going dependability. Jordan had been in the same job for twelve years, and she could set her clock accurately by his departure and arrival. With her judgment glasses on, she started seeing him as boring and lacking in ambition. During their courtship she had loved his flexibity and willingness to go along with all her suggestions. Through her judgment blinders she saw him as spineless and weak, without an original thought in his head.

Marilyn divorced Jordan and married Steve who was very aggressive, ambitious, and had strong opinions. At first Marilyn admired these virtues in Steve, and felt lucky to be married to an exciting man who knew what he wanted and where he was going. She felt protected and taken care of. Later she saw him as controlling and unyielding because he would not do what she wanted him to do. Instead of feeling protected, she felt dominated and not taken seriously.

Marilyn divorced Steve and married another man like Jordan. She is now on her seventh marriage because she does not see that she loses her good feelings and happiness every time she puts on her blinders of judgment and expectation. She believes she sees reality through her blinders. **Love does not judge differences.**

MYTH NO. 2
IT IS IMPORTANT TO BE COMPATIBLE

Dolores divorced Scott. Her explanation, "We just were not compatible."

Regarding marriage, there is a pervasive distortion of the meaning of compatibility. The distortion is the notion that compatibility means two people must have the same beliefs and interests in order to live together harmoniously.

When we understand separate realities we can see that it is not possible for two people to be the same. Couples who are fooled into thinking they have the same interests and beliefs get into trouble when they later find that what they thought was the same is not exactly the same.

Dolores and Scott were delighted to discover that they both enjoyed tennis. They were already in love, but saw their mutual interest in tennis as proof that they were *compatible*.

The trouble started when Scott learned that Dolores liked to play more often than he did. He thought she took it too seriously. Dolores assumed anyone who was really interested in tennis would feel exactly the same way she did about it. They both felt cheated and misunderstood. The only solution they could see, since they were obviously not as compatible as they thought, was divorce.

Do you find it hard to believe that anyone would get a divorce because they didn't feel exactly the same about tennis? Any beliefs about incompatibility do not make any more sense than this example.

The true meaning of compatibility is having the ability to live together in harmony. We all have this ability. Compatibility is a natural state when we dismiss negative thoughts and respect differences instead of judging them.

It is not important to be compatible in the way that is commonly defined today. We don't need to have the same interests and beliefs. We have compatibility when we see differences with love, interest, understanding, respect, and acceptance. We are compatible when we are sharing good feelings rather than judgments and expectations. We are naturally compatible when we are experiencing life through our clear channels rather than through our thought systems.

MYTH NO 3
IT IS IMPORTANT TO COMMUNICATE
ABOUT PROBLEMS

There is also a pervasive distortion of the meaning of communication in marriage. How often have you heard these statements? "We just can't communicate." Or, "The key to a good relationship is communication."

The distortion in these statements is the implication that it is important to make your partner understand and accept what you feel and what you believe. If you can get your partner to believe your reality rather than his or her own, then you have succeeded in good communication.

This is the same as saying, "You should be able to have the same reality I have. No more separate reality for you. Also, you should have the same thought system I have, including all my particular judgments, expectations, and desires. You should have my illusions, not your own."

No wonder almost everyone is failing in their attempts at good communication. It is impossible for your partner to believe your reality rather than his or her own. With understanding he or she might dismiss both realities for the illusions of thought that they are. Until then they would rather fight than switch.

We are always communicating, either from our distorted thought system or from our clear thought channel. Since we are always communicating, the important thing is to know where our communication is coming from. When we are communicating from our thought systems, we are sharing negative feelings, thoughts, and beliefs. Even sulky or angry silences are communication. When we are communicating from our clear channel we are sharing the positive feelings we experience through inspiration, common sense, and wisdom.

Sharing positive feelings is often done silently. Many couples do more quiet touching and less verbal communication when they realize how inadequate words are to express beautiful feelings.

When we are in a state of happiness and peace of mind, it is amazing how much we can enjoy what is usually referred to as mundane information. "Is dinner ready?" "I paid the bills today." "How are the kids?" "Shall we go to the beach?" Communication becomes light and easy, not heavy in the sense that we communicate, to get it all out, or to make sure our partner knows how we feel (from our thought system).

This may sound boring to some people. Happiness and peace of mind are not boring. In that state of mind it is common to feel so full of the joy of living and love for our partners that we sometimes wonder how we can handle it all.

Is another should or shouldn't creeping into your thoughts? Are you wondering, "Does this mean we should not talk about our separate realities?"

What we do is not the point. Talking about our separate realities, or not talking about them, is simply a different experience when we understand the principles. You will probably feel a sense of humor when talking about separate realities, instead of taking them seriously.

MYTH NO. 4
NEVER GO TO SLEEP UNTIL
YOU HAVE RESOLVED AN ARGUMENT

Sometimes the best way to dismiss thoughts of right and wrong is some kind of cooling off period to help us get quiet. This could be sleeping it off, a walk around the block, or anything else that helps us feel better.

Kate and Frank believed they should never go to sleep until they had resolved their arguments. They would stand toe to toe and argue about who was right and who was wrong. Since they were both caught up in their individual thought systems and separate realities, it was impossible to hear each other or solve anything. Since they believed they should be able to solve their arguments, their frustrations would build. Frank would finally leave, slamming the door behind him and go to the nearest bar. Kate would go to bed, but couldn't sleep because she was furiously thinking about their failure to solve the problem before going to sleep.

They went to see a therapist who taught them about the principles. It became obvious to them what they could do.

Frank said to Kate, "Since I like to leave the house when I am upset, I will leave, but I won't slam the door, and I won't go to a bar. I will take a walk around the block until my thought system is tucked away where it can't hurt me, and I am able to enjoy how much I love you again. You can know that my leaving is not anger at you, but just my own recognition that I'm caught up in negative thoughts and need to get quiet until they go away."

Kate said, "Since I enjoy going to bed, that is what I will do. However, instead of continuing to think about my negative thoughts, I will read a book or go to sleep with the peace-provoking knowledge that they are just thoughts. You can know I'm not going to bed to get away from you, but to rest until the negative thoughts are gone and nothing is left but wisdom and common sense."

MYTH NO. 5
IF YOU ARE NOT HAVING FIGHTS YOU ARE NOT GOING DEEP IN YOUR RELATIONSHIP -- OR SOMEONE IS GIVING IN TOO MUCH

Couples who understand the principles of psychological functioning that underlie their separate realities do not fight, or realize they are off track when they do.

Sylvia shared, "I can't remember the last time Tim and I had a fight. It has been at least four years. We had lots of fights before. We just enjoy each other now."

Scott shared, "Lisa and I still have fights, but they are all silent. We know we are just in a low mood, or lost in our thought systems if we feel like fighting, so we keep quiet and wait for it to pass."

Beth shared, "Tom and I used to have fights and lose respect for each other. We still have fights once in a while, but now we lose respect for the fights instead of for each other."

Kathie shared, "When Dave and I have fights now, we can't take them seriously, so we end up laughing. It is especially fun to watch my Sarah Bernhardt act while I am still taking things a little bit seriously."

I used to get really upset when I wanted to discuss something my husband and I disagreed about, and he would tell me, "Forget it."

I would retort, "What do you mean, forget it? If you had any sensitivity at all, you would be upset too." Now I say, "Thanks for reminding me."

MYTH NO. 6
WE WILL BE HAPPY WHEN OUR CIRCUMSTANCES CHANGE (WHEN WE HAVE MORE MONEY, OR A HOUSE, OR CHILDREN, OR NO CHILDREN, OR WHEN YOU CHANGE)

Happiness is a state of mind that has nothing to do with circumstances.

Dear Abby received a letter from a woman who was complaining about her husband's snoring. Dear Abby included another letter from a woman who stated, "I used to complain about snoring. My husband is dead now. I would give anything to be able to hear him snoring again."

A popular story is the one we hear over and over about struggling newlyweds who do not appreciate the joy of being together and in love because they keep focusing on how much better it will be when they have more money, a house, and furniture. Then they get the money, the house, and furniture and don't enjoy it because they think they are not as much in love as they used to be. They are not as much in love as they used to be because they keep focusing on circumstances and miss the joy of what is. They cannot see what is when focusing on what is not.

We feel dissatisfaction in a relationship when we are focusing on what we think we should be getting to satisfy our beliefs about how things should be. When we recognize what we are doing to create this dissatisfaction, we can see that these beliefs are always connected to our illusionary ego and self-importance.

We have satisfaction, peace of mind, and happiness in our relationships when we are loving unconditionally -- when we take off our blinders and see our partner the same way we did when we fell in love in the first place.

You might object, "But my wife is not the same as when we fell in love. She wasn't fat then." The answer to every objection you might have can be found in the principles.

Your happiness has nothing to do with what anyone else is or does. If you are seeing the fat, you are not seeing the insecurity, which you may have helped create. *When you see with* **love** *instead of* **judgment,** *you will also see solutions.*

June was very unhappy because her husband, Cy, was an alcoholic. She vowed to herself that if he did not stop drinking by the time the children left home, she would leave him. They had been married 30 years when the last child left for college.

Before June kept her vow, she decided to pray about it. She was surprised at the clear inspiration she received, "It is not your province to judge your husband, it is your province to love your husband unconditionally."

105

June's reality changed. She did love Cy unconditionally, without effort. Within three months Cy stopped
drinking.

MYTH NO. 7
WHEN YOU LOVE SOMEONE, IT IS NATURAL TO FEEL INSECURE. JEALOUSY IS A SIGN THAT YOU CARE

Jealousy is nothing more than insecurity produced by
thoughts about ego and self-importance. These insecurities
usually take the form of some kind of vulnerability fear: fear
of inadequacy, fear of rejection, or fear of powerlessness.

All these fears are illusions based on taking thoughts
of ego and self-importance seriously, yet many people base
their lives on these illusions. They waste all kinds of time
and energy trying to hide their fears, or trying to blame
themselves or others as the cause of their fears.

Fears of inadequacy take such forms as. "I won't be
good enough. Someone else will be better than I am. If
only I were more beautiful, more handsome, more powerful,
more successful, more intelligent, more witty; then I would
be ok."

Fears of rejection take such forms as, "He won't care
as much as I care, which means I'm not good enough,
which means he might leave me, which means I will be
alone and will never find anyone else."

Fears of powerlessness take such forms as, "I can't
do anything about this. I have no control over what is
happening to me, I can't make someone love me."

Self-esteem is a natural state of being when it is not
weighted down with thoughts that produce the illusion of
insecurity. The following poem illustrates the kind of crazy
thoughts and feelings that can be produced when taking
thoughts of insecurity seriously.

SELF-ESTEEM

Self-esteem --
such an elusive concept.

Understanding it
intellectually
is not so difficult.

Of course I'm ok
just as I am.
Certainly it doesn't matter
what anyone else thinks.

Then why do I feel
this pit
in my stomach
when I think
you might not care
enough?
(What is enough?)

Why am I afraid
to care
too much?
(What is too much?)
For fear
you might not care
as much
(What is as much?)

Of course self-esteem is an elusive concept -- it is an illusion based on the illusion of ego. How could anyone lack self-esteem without thinking they don't have self-esteem? Then can you imagine trying to build self-esteem, when working from a premise that you don't have it.

The belief that anyone can lack self-worth is an extremely silly thought. However, the illusions created by silly thoughts are powerful detours away from happiness when they are seen as reality.

Bill and Sue went to a party. Bill became very angry when he saw Sue dancing with another man. On the way home Bill sulked until Sue was able to persuade him to admit something was wrong. Then he blew! He blamed her for flirting and accused her of being very inconsiderate. He would not accept her explanation that she didn't even want to dance with the other man, but didn't know how to refuse gracefully.

Bill had become so lost in the contents of his thinking that he didn't connect his behavior with his original thoughts of insecurity. He had jumped to blame to cover up his thoughts of all the vulnerability fears. He was afraid Sue might find him inadequate compared to the other man, that she might decide to reject him, and he felt powerless to do anything about it. Expressing anger gave him a false sense of power and control -- not happiness.

Bill decided to leave Sue to protect himself from being left by her. Bill's thinking is illustrated in the following poem.

PERPETUATION

I keep worrying
that you
will reject me.

That would be
terrible
because
I love being with you.

Isn't it crazy
that to keep you
from rejecting me
I get defensive (offensive)
and reject you?

So
I save myself
from possible rejection
but the results
are the same
I can't be with you.

And
it is
  terrible!

Is that called
  perpetuating
    what you fear?

Insecurity has nothing to do with reality. It is all based on negative thoughts which are seen as real. Look at the unhappiness Bill created when he took those thoughts seriously. He gave up his happiness for some crazy thoughts.

It would have been much simpler for Bill to dismiss his negative thoughts instead of dismissing his marriage.

MYTH NO. 8
YOU HAVE TO HAVE A RELATIONSHIP

Who says?

This myth is just another belief based on another thought. When you look at the evidence, it doesn't make sense. There are just as many unhappy people in relationships as there are happy people in relationships. (Actually statistics show more people in relationships who are unhappy than happy, but I'm presenting principles, not facts.) And, there are just as many people who are happy even though they don't have a relationship, as there are people who are unhappy because they don't have a relationship.

It is all thought, not circumstances.

When we have peace of mind, gratitude, and satisfaction with all that IS, we don't see what is not. We are happy with or without a relationship.

We can be in love with life, alone.

Chapter 13

CHILDREN

Parents all chuckle and feel a bond when they hear, "Aren't children wonderful -- when they are asleep?"

Understanding will help you *see* your children as wonderful most of the time. When you don't see them as wonderful, you will know it is not them, but you, being caught up in your thought system.

I have written a book entitled *Positive Discipline.** This book is full of common sense and wisdom for working with children in effective and loving ways. However, before understanding the principles taught in this book, I often turned the common sense and wisdom into rules and shoulds, and felt like a failure when I did not follow them.

The *understanding* I have now makes it easier to *see* the deeper wisdom and principle behind the suggestions in *Positive Discipline.* From a happy state of mind, following these suggestions is natural rather than an effort. When I don't follow common sense and wisdom, I forgive myself, learn from my mistakes, and use recovery to clean up the mess I created from using my thought system.

Some of the information in this chapter and the next chapter is adopted or adapted from *Positive Discipline.*

EXAMPLE IS THE BEST TEACHER

Have you ever noticed how many *unhappy* parents are telling their children what they *must* do in order to be successful and happy. These parents are often filled with stress, anxiety, and other forms thought-produced insecurity as they follow false promises from their thought systems for finding happiness outside themselves.

**Positive Discipline* by Jane Nelsen

Many parents have not taken a close look at their own lives, or they would *see* why so many children are rebelling today. By the time children become teenagers they begin to see discrepancies between what we say and how we live. They see parents who live in unhappiness and other forms of dissatisfaction as they try to *prove themselves* based on *society's* notions of *success*. No wonder teenagers do not have much respect for the *establishment*.

When we take a closer look, it becomes obvious that *success* has become more important than happiness. In fact, happiness is often sacrificed for the illusion of success.

At a deep *feeling* level many teenagers know this does not make sense, and they rebel. The problem is that their rebellion is often based on thoughts that create other forms of insecurity, and they choose a lifestyle that does not bring any greater happiness than that of their parents.

Other teenagers conform and join in the illusion of trying to live up to *society's* notions of success.

With *understanding,* parents can live a truly happy life. They can create an atmosphere of common sense and wisdom and show their children how to do the same. Children will want to follow the example of parents who have this feeling.

When we become happy parents, our children will become happy children. When we follow common sense and wisdom, our children will follow common sense and wisdom.

In Chapter six I told the story of my reactions, both from my thought system and from my clear channel, when my son Mark was suspended from school for having cigarettes in his locker. I left it up to your imagination as to what might have happened if I had taken my judgmental thoughts seriously instead of dismissing them and following inspiration from my common sense and wisdom.

Now I will tell you what did happen. Mark made friends with some boys interested in bike racing. He and his new friends spend most of their free time in an empty field building mounds and jumping their bikes.

Mark occasionally associates with his friends who smoke and drink, but follows his own common sense. He confided in me, "They don't even ask me if I want to smoke anymore because they know I will say no."

Children will find their own sanity when they experience sanity from their parents. When they experience insanity (crazy thinking) from their parents, they seem to prefer their own insanity. Actually, far too many adopt the insanity of their parents and pass it on from generation to generation.

FEEDING FIRES

Children often start harmless little fires that would quickly burn out if adults didn't feed the flames until they become roaring bonfires.

Every Christmas my children have complained after all the presents have been opened, "Is that all?"

My thoughts would go crazy over issues of selfishness, lack of gratitude, spoiled bratness, and I would start my lecture, "It doesn't matter how much we do for you kids, it is never enough. Next Christmas everyone is going to get one present, period, and we'll spend the rest of the day in an orphanage so you can see what it is like to not have anything."

We would all end up feeling bad about Christmas and each other.

Last Christmas I heard, "Is that all?"

I replied, "I can remember having that feeling when I was a little girl."

There was an incredulous, "Really? Then how come you call us spoiled when we say it?"

I answered, "Temporary insanity."

The children laughed and went off to enjoy their new possessions.

A friend recently shared that she once had the same problem. (This type of thing goes on in thousands of households.) She said, "Last Christmas I totally ignored the remark (did not feed the flame at all) and noticed it was only seconds until my little girl acted like she had never felt any disappointment and was playing with her toys."

IN THE BEGINNING

Babies come into this world with clear channels which have not been blocked by a thought system. They do not have memories of the past, or thoughts of the future.

They smile when are happy, and cry when they want something.

They are curious and give their full attention to whatever they are interested in. They stare, without embarrassment, at anything or anyone new. They have natural learning abilities. They effortlessly learn a language and many other things without *thinking* about it.

Toddlers are not worried about making mistakes while learning to walk. Can you imagine what would happen if they had negative thoughts every time they fell down? "Oh dear, I failed again. I am not a very good person. I better not try again, or I might fall again." They don't think those kind of thoughts until adults start giving them those kinds of ideas. We don't follow our own common sense and allow our children to do the same. Instead we start teaching them all kinds of rules of behavior along with the crazy idea that self-worth depends on how well they obey the rules.

It may sound like I am advocating permissiveness. Following inspiration (which will let us know exactly how much guidance our children need and how to do it) and allowing children to do the same, is nothing like permissiveness. Children often lose access to their natural common sense because they love us so much that they accept what we tell them, whether or not it comes from common sense and wisdom.

YES OR NO

When coming from inspiration we know which answer is appropriate to our children's requests.

I used to say "yes" out of guilt, or "no" out of insecurity. In other words, the basis for my answers would be something like, "I should say 'yes' to make up for past neglect. I should say 'yes' or they might get mad at me. I better say 'yes' because I can't handle the hassle right now. I have to say 'no' or they might get spoiled. I have to say 'no' because they might take advantage of me if I say 'yes.' I better say 'no' or they will expect 'yes' all the time."

It is amazing how little hassle I get when I follow inspiration from my common sense before I answer yes or no. I have noticed I don't say no as often because of some future possibility. And when I do say no, it is with a feeling of love and sometimes humor that it is accepted in the same spirit.

LISTEN DEEPLY

If we are hearing something that is making us feel upset, we are not listening deeply enough. We are reacting (from ego) to the words rather than to the insecurity behind the words. When we hear the feeling level, we will be inspired to respond lovingly.

The minute I came into the house one day, after being away for a few days, Mary started barraging me with, "Take me here. Take me there."

I wanted to let her know how unrealistic she was being, that I was tired, that all she cared about was what I could *do* for her instead of being glad to see me, and that she needed to be more considerate.

Then I started listening deeper and could see that she just wanted to be with me. I said, "Let's sit down and plan something we can do together at a time convenient for both of us." Mary immediately calmed down.

MISTAKES

Mistakes do not matter. They are simply opportunities to learn. So what if we think a negative thought and act on it? So what if we get into a low mood and yell at our children? Recovery is just an insight away.

Getting off track is nothing to get upset about when we know what causes it and what to do about it. I call this:

RECOVERY.

Mrs. Lamont tells how she used recovery after dealing with a situation from craziness. She found a six pack of beer in fourteen-year-old Marie's closet. When Marie came home, she met her at the door with the case of beer in hand, and in an accusing voice demanded, "What is this?"

Marie sarcastically replied, "It looks like a six pack of beer to me."

Mrs. Lamont snapped back, "Don't get smart with me, young lady. I found this in the bottom of your closet."

Marie remembered, "Oh, I had forgotten all about that. I was hiding it for a friend."

"Do you expect me to believe that?"

"I don't care if you believe it or not," Marie shouted as she ran to her room.

Mrs. Lamont called after her, "You are grounded for a week, Miss Smart Mouth."

Mrs. Lamont shared this incident with her friend, Lillian, who helped her get back in touch with her common sense by asking her, "Why were you upset about the beer?"

Mrs. Lamont (still caught up in her thought system) indignantly replied, "Because I don't want her to get into trouble."

Lillian could see that her friend had still lost sight of her common sense reasons, and gently suggested, "I think you have forgotten the real reason you don't want her to get into trouble."

Mrs. Lamont finally understood and replied sheepishly, "You mean because I love her. I can see now that I did not let that message get through. Thanks, Lillian. I know what to do now."

That evening Mrs. Lamont sat down with Marie, "I'm sorry for the way I acted yesterday. I said some pretty silly things."

"That's okay, Mom. I really was hiding it for a friend."

"Marie, I really love you. Sometimes I get scared when I have thoughts that you might hurt yourself. Then I forget to tell you I love you and just blurt out my craziness."

Marie started to cry and said, "I have been feeling like I was just a big problem to you and that only my friends like me."

"I can see how you could get that impression from my behavior. Can we start over?"

Mrs. Lamont finished her story, "I don't know if Marie will drink beer or not, but I know I am not now increasing the chances that she will because of the insecurity she feels about our relationship."

Children are so forgiving. They may be feeling resentment or rebellion when we are humiliating them, but as soon as we say we are sorry they are quick to say, "That's okay."

Recovery can be a beautiful way to make a relationship even nicer than it was before. *Recovery* is natural when we dismiss negative thoughts and see the situation with new perspective.

ENJOY YOUR CHILDREN

I have a great idea for a book on childrearing with a guarantee that would make it a best seller. The guarantee would state: If you don't experience wonderful results *after following the advice* in this $10 book for one year, you will receive 100 times your money back. In other words, satisfaction or $1000.00. (This guarantee is backed by Lloyd's of London.)

I think people would be stampeding the bookstores -- even after they learned that the book contained only three words.

Would you like to know what those three words would be?

Enjoy your children.

When we are enjoying our children we will experience fantastic results in all areas of concern regarding childrearing. What to do to achieve positive results will be natural and easy from this state of mind, even though *what to do* may be different for each parent.

When children fight, one parent may join them in a good natured wrestling match. Another parent may say, "This doesn't look like fun to me. I think I'll take a walk around the block until you are finished." Another parent may lose his happy state of mind and punish the children, and then use *recovery* as soon as he regains his happy state of mind. Another parent may hold a *peace conference* as soon as the children are ready. The possibilities are unlimited for every possible situation when you enjoy your children.

When we are following the inspiration from our common sense and wisdom, it is natural to love and enjoy our children and to know what to do when they need guidance. When children experience this kind of atmosphere, how can they go wrong? They will probably still establish a thought system, and they will get caught up in it sometimes and do things that don't produce positive results. However, they will have learned from us how to get back on course to lead a happy life.

Provide a good feeling level and all problems will take care of themselves. This does not mean you will never have to do anything. It means that when you are feeling good you will know what to do for positive results.

Chapter 14

MYTHS OF CHILDREARING

Parents want their children to be happy and *successful.* Some interesting myths have been created through well-meaning efforts regarding the best way to help children achieve success and happiness.

MYTH NO. 1
PUNISHMENT TEACHES CHILDREN TO IMPROVE THEIR BEHAVIOR

Where did we ever get the crazy idea that in order to make children do better, first we have to make them feel worse. Making children feel bad lowers their mood or level of consciousness so they don't do better. They do better when they feel good.

Parents punish because of thought-created insecurity in the form of fear of failure (their children's and their own), a mistaken belief that punishment will help, and not having access to inspiration from their common sense and wisdom.

Punishment comes from a lower level of consciousness, beliefs from the thought system, and not respecting separate realities. Children usually react to punishment from their own thought system in one of the three forms:

THE THREE R'S OF PUNISHMENT

1. Resentment ("This is unfair.")
2. Revenge ("They are winning now, but I'll get even.")
3. Retreat:
   a. Rebellion ("I won't get caught next time.")
   b. Insecurity ("I am a bad person.")

Punishment is one of the ways we teach children to program their thought system and to live from that source, rather than from their common sense.

Children who are punished do not come to their parents when they have questions about life. Children come to parents who interact with them from common sense and wisdom. Parents who interact with their children from their common sense and wisdom will know what to do to teach their children with love, understanding, and compassion.

MYTH NO. 2
CHILDREN NEED TO LEARN OBEDIENCE

Children will not be helped by learning obedience. They will be helped when they are taught to follow the inspiration from their common sense and wisdom, which will never lead them astray.

When they are babies, they need supervision and guidance. That is not the same as obedience. Supervision and guidance are based on feelings of love and concern for the safety and well-being of our children. When parents stay in touch with their common sense and wisdom from their clear channels, they will know how to guide their children in ways that will achieve positive results. When children experience examples of common sense and wisdom, that is what they will follow when they grow beyond the need for guidance and supervision.

A toddler does not have enough information and understanding to stay out of the path of moving cars. But a toddler is not capable of understanding obedience about that either.

It is very popular for parents to insist that they must punish their children with a spanking to teach them obedience about staying out of the street. I ask these parents, "After you have given your children a spanking for running into the street, will you then let them play by themselves near a busy street?"

I have never found a parent who said yes. Punishment does not help children stay out of the street. It is more helpful to teach them to look both ways to see if a car is coming before crossing a street. Children need supervision while they are young, along with common sense information that they can rely on when they are more mature.

Not teaching obedience does not mean permissiveness. Many families teach common sense responsibility and cooperation by having family meetings where the children take part in handling most potential problem situations such as doing chores, homework and disagreements. These families work together to decide on solutions that make sense to everyone.

Use and teach common sense rather than obedience.

MYTH NO. 3
BE A PARENT, NOT A FRIEND TO YOUR CHILDREN

I am not really sure what that myth means, but it sounds ominous. It makes parenting sound like such an unfriendly chore where you must remain superior and aloof.

It can be such fun to share life with children. It doesn't make sense not to enjoy them as we discover who they are. Parents often tell their children who they should be, instead of discovering and enjoying who they are.

One of the reasons we enjoy being around friends is because they love us unconditionally. They are usually very good at helping us see things from common sense and wisdom instead of our programed thought system. Just being around a friend can raise our mood or level of consciousness.

There need not be any difference between being a parent and being a friend. Children want and appreciate advice when it comes from common sense and wisdom. They are confused or rebellious when advice comes from a thought system. Just like friends, they want unconditional love and acceptance, not judgment.

Children will learn more from us when we interact with them the way we do with friends.

MYTH NO. 4
PROBLEMS MUST BE DEALT WITH IMMEDIATELY

Use your feelings as a compass to let you know when to deal with a problem. If you are upset, you know you are caught up in your thought system. Anything you do from that state of mind will not achieve positive results. It can be very helpful to let your children know you need *time out* or *a cooling off period* before you can talk about the situation.

Mr. Stewart had an interesting way of calling for time out. He would exaggerate his feelings and jokingly say to his son, Andrew, "If you don't run, I'll probably clobber you."

Andrew would run. When they both felt better, after a cooling off period, they would get back together and solve the problem with common sense.

Understanding helps us know when we are in a low mood, and to dismiss our thoughts and be quiet until it passes. When we forget, and do something with our children that doesn't feel good, it can always be *fixed* through **recovery** when we are in a better mood.

MYTH NO. 5
WHAT OTHER PEOPLE THINK ABOUT YOUR PARENTING SKILLS IS IMPORTANT

I remember claiming once that to be a good mother was one of the most important things in life to me. A wise and observant friend asked, "In whose eyes? The neighbors' or your children's?"

The question hit me like a ton of bricks as I realized how much I did as a mother to seek approval from others. With that as a motive, I would not follow my common sense to get the best results with my children.

Social pressure is just another thought. It cannot hurt us unless we take it seriously. Wanting to live up to our imagined expectations of others is an *ego trip* that will definitely interfere with common sense and wisdom.

One summer, when Mark was ten years old, we went backpacking with several friends. Mark was a very good sport and carried his pack the long, six miles into the canyon. When we were getting ready for the long, steep trek back out, Mark complained about how uncomfortable his pack was.

His dad jokingly remarked, "You can take it. You are the son of a Marine."

Mark did not think that was very funny, since it did not solve his problem, but he started the climb anyway. He had not gone very far ahead of us when we heard his pack come crashing down the hill toward us.

I thought he had fallen and called out, "Mark! Are you okay? What happened?"

Mark angrily called back, "Nothing, it hurts!" He continued climbing without his pack.

The rest of the group watched with interest. One adult offered to carry his pack for him.

My thoughts went crazy, "What are people going to think? They are all wondering if I can make *Positive Discipline* work. What if I can't? They will think I'm terrible if I just let Mark *get away* with that."

I dismissed those thoughts and remembered I was more interested in Mark than in what other people thought.

I asked the rest of the party to hike on ahead so we could handle this in private. I then did the best I could to understand Mark's reality and asked, "Did you think we didn't care when we didn't pay serious attention when you tried to tell us your pack hurt before we even started?"

Mark said, "Yes, and I'm not going to carry it."

Dad said, "I'm sorry, son. Will you give me another chance?"

Mark agreed, and they figured out a way to stuff his coat over the sore part to cushion the pack. Mark carried the pack the rest of the way with only a few, minor complaints.

We have found that our children always respond positively to sanity. They are very forgiving and cooperative when we recognize that we have made a mistake and follow our common sense to correct it.

MYTH NO. 6
CHILDREN SHOULD BE SEEN AND NOT HEARD

That may sound like an old-fashioned myth that is not prevalent today. We claim to care about what children have to say, but how often do we really *understand* the separate realities of our children? How often do we punish first and ask questions later?

When Kenny was seven, Bradley five, and Lisa three, my husband and I took them with us while looking at building lots. Bradley and Kenny complained the whole time about how hot and boring it was. Lisa played quietly on my lap or took a nap.

The next day we wanted to continue our search. We thought we were doing Kenny and Bradley a big favor by leaving them with the neighbors who had children their age. We planned to take Lisa with us because she had not been a problem.

When we started to leave, Kenny said, "I want to go."

I said, "No you don't. Remember how much you complained about how hot and boring it was yesterday."

Kenny said, "I don't care. I want to go."

I insisted that he did not really want to go, and we left without him.

When we returned home we saw that he had taken a knife and slashed the material on Lisa's high chair. I spanked him and sent him to his room.

In a few hours I was in a better mood and was able to guess what Kenny might have been thinking. I went into his room and checked it out with him. "Kenny, did you think that because we took Lisa with us, and not you, that we loved her more than we love you?"

"Yes," Kenny sobbed.

I shared, "I can guess what that felt like. I had a similar thing happen to me. When I was ten, my Mother took my older sister to New York City. She said I couldn't go because I was not old enough, but I thought it was because she loved my sister more than me."

Kenny responded, "Really?"

I asked, "Would you like to know how I felt about not taking you with us?"

Kenny nodded, so I proceeded, "I love you very much. I didn't want you to be hot and bored. I thought you would have much more fun playing with your friends than being cooped up in the car."

He grinned happily. Kenny could now hear my reality in this atmosphere of love and understanding.

I went on, "Now we need to do something about the highchair. Do you have any ideas?"

Kenny enthusiastically claimed, "I can fix it!"

I agreed, "I'll bet you can."

Kenny took fifty cents from his allowance. We went to a store, found a remnant, and stapled a new covering on the highchair.

You could call this **recovery,** as explained in the last chapter, but be careful about looking at anything as a technique. It was simply the results of *understanding* that came from dismissing negative thoughts so that my level of consciousness was raised and I could see the situation with perspective.

From a higher level of consciousness, we know through inspiration what to do to create feelings of love and understanding. With love and understanding, problems are solved, and we enjoy a beautiful relationship

PART FOUR

KEYS TO WISDOM

Chapter 15

WISDOM FROM THE AGES

Wisdom from the ages makes sense at a deeper level when we understand the principles of thinking as a function, separate realities, levels of consciousness, and feelings as a compass.

IF YOU CAN'T SAY SOMETHING NICE, DON'T SAY ANYTHING AT ALL

It is easy to *see* the wisdom in this when we know our reality is just a creation of our thoughts, rather than *the right* reality. It doesn't make sense to say something nasty or judgmental about other realities. Since negative feelings are simply an indicator of a low mood and not seeing things with perspective and understanding, it is wise not to say anything at all during that time.

As soon as we dismiss our negative thoughts, seeing or saying something unkind will not be part of our reality.

COUNT TO TEN

This is just another way of dismissing thought and getting quiet until low moods pass. Some of us may need to count to ten thousand before we **see** with clarity and perspective.

HASTE MAKES WASTE

This makes sense when we know that the need to hurry and figure things out keeps us bogged down in our thought system. We gain perspective when we slow down and leave room for inspiration.

STICKS AND STONES CAN BREAK MY BONES, BUT NAMES CAN NEVER HURT ME

Shari said, "I feel like a failure because my husband tells me I never do anything right. No wonder I don't have any self-esteem."

Shari's feelings have nothing to do with what her husband says. It is her thoughts about what her husband says that create her feelings. If Shari would dismiss her thoughts about what her husband says, she would see with perspective. She would understand that what her husband says comes from his separate reality. She would see the innocence and insecurity behind what he is saying. If he had *understanding* he would not have negative feelings and perceptions which he feels he needs to express.

With *understanding* Shari would know what to do. Instead of taking his thoughts seriously, she could let them pass *right over her thought system.* She might then feel inspired to hug him, make a joke, take a walk, or whatever her common sense would lead her to do.

A STITCH IN TIME SAVES NINE

The only stitch we need take is to *understand* thought. The trouble this will save us is greater than nine.

A small tear in cloth gets larger and larger unless it is stitched while it is still small. A negative thought can get more and more powerful unless in is dismissed as soon as you *realize* it is just a thought.

LACK OF WISDOM FROM THE AGES

An understanding of the principles also helps us *see* the lack of wisdom in some of the old adages.

IDLENESS IS THE DEVIL'S WORKSHOP

The opposite is true. Idleness leaves room for inspiration.

So many people are afraid that if they are not constantly *busy* they will not be productive. We need to take a closer look at *productiveness.* Productivity from inspiration will produce happiness. Productivity from the thought system produces unhappiness. We may be productive in achievement, financial success, or a spotless house, while our personal or family life is falling apart.

Actually, it is never what we do that matters, but why we do it, and the results we achieve. When we are idle because we are happy and want to just enjoy life, we will find more happiness. When we are idle because we are unhappy, that takes the form of depression or boredom, and we become more unhappy.

It is a popular opinion today that watching television is a waste of time. Maybe so, maybe not. We can watch television as part of our enjoyment of life, or as an effort to escape life. We can avoid watching television because we are afraid of what other people will think (instead of trusting our own wisdom) or because we have adopted a belief that, "Only uneducated people who don't have anything better to do watch television."

The same could be said of any activity or inactivity in life. When happiness and peace of mind is our only direction, we will know what to do regardless of what anyone else has ever thought or said.

THE ROAD TO HELL IS PAVED WITH GOOD INTENTIONS

Everyone has good intentions. Everyone wants to be happy. It is the thought system that distorts good intentions. Everyone does the best they can based on their present level of understanding.

Forgiveness is easy when we *understand* the good intentions of ourselves and others rather than paying attention to the behavior resulting from the insecurities produced by a distorted thought system.

A person who is locked into their thought system and negative behavior has created a kind of hell. It is our judgments of them that lead to our own kind of hell.

A PERSON WITHOUT GOALS IS LIKE A BOAT WITHOUT A RUDDER

A person with goals is more like a boat with a rudder stuck in one position. Being without goals allows us to enjoy opportunities as they come along.

The belief that we must have goals is based on thoughts that create insecurity such as, "Without goals we will never accomplish anything." People who have goals based on those thoughts do not accomplish happiness. These people often reach their goals and quickly invent new ones so they won't feel useless if they are not accomplishing something. They feel only temporary satisfaction.

When we are not focused on *goals* for the sake of achievement, we will see *opportunities* for the sake of enjoyment. Productivity is enhanced through enjoyment. With understanding we want to accomplish only those things that are enhancing, rather than the things that satisfy our illusionary ego or a need to live up to the judgments of others.

ANYTHING WORTH DOING IS WORTH DOING WELL

This could be true if *well* simply means that you enjoy it. However, *well* is usually a judgment, with implications of perfection. Beliefs about perfection often takes the joy out of doing.

How many people will not sing for the fun of it because they feel they can not sing well enough? This is just one example of the many things people will not do for the pleasure of the doing because of the fear of not living up to the judgment of doing it *well*.

Anything worth doing, is worth doing for the fun of it.

GROWTH IS PAINFUL

It is true that what is referred to as *growth* within the thought system is painful. Coping is stressful, but it is seen as growth. Delving into the past, expressing *feelings* or anger, overcoming *obstacles*, controlling *emotions*, is very painful. This is not growth -- it is crazy.

Growth based on inspiration from common sense and wisdom is not painful. It is painless to dismiss thoughts upon which the pain is based.

We are completely satisfied when we *see* life with *understanding,* but it keeps getting better because our understanding continues to grow and deepen. There is nothing painful about it.

IT IS TOO GOOD TO BE TRUE

The only thing that can take the goodness away is negative thoughts. Think it, and you have it.

If we think something can't last, it is because we have quit enjoying what is and have adopted thoughts such as, "I can't be happy if I don't have this," or, "It might not last," or "I don't deserve it."

GOOD THINGS ALWAYS COME TO AN END

When we think, "Good things always come to an end," we have put on our blinders so we can't see the abundance of good things.

Good things don't come to an end until we change our thoughts and start worrying about the past or future and quit enjoying what is. When we see the abundance of good things, it does not make sense to worry about losing one good thing.

From our clear channels we will see what is with gratitude.

Life is good!

Chapter 16

KEYS TO HAPPINESS -- A SUMMARY

Would you like to be in prison? Would you knowingly confine yourself to a lifetime sentence in a dungeon?

You have probably locked yourself in a prison without even knowing you are there. Your thought system creates a prison that is more confining that any dungeon.

The prison walls you create in your mind are formed from illusionary thoughts, but they can be more binding than concrete.

The foundation stones for the illusionary but confining prison of the mind are made of thoughts which create feelings of insecurity. The walls are made of whatever form the insecurity takes -- self-importance, drinking, anxiety, overeating, judgments, over-achievement, expectations, stress, dissatisfaction, depression, blame. The ceiling is the belief that these thoughts are reality.

Understanding, realization, insight, awareness are the keys that crumble the prison walls. Know the truth, and the truth shall make you free.

The first key to happiness is *realizing* that thinking is a function. This realization is the key to experiencing natural mental health. Those who believe that the contents of their thinking is an external reality, often experience stress, anxiety, and other forms of insecurity. They take negative thoughts seriously, turn them into beliefs, and live for them.

Those who *understand* that thinking is a function (and know they can think anything they want) experience peace of mind. They see the humor in their negative creations and do not take them seriously. They are then able to dismiss the negativity and experience natural well being.

To say it another way -- anytime we are feeling bad for any reason, it is because we have forgotten that thinking is a function and see our thoughts as reality.

COMMON EXCUSES FOR FORGETTING
THAT THINKING IS A FUNCTION

Circumstances

It is never the circumstances, but only our thoughts about them. We can always find examples of people who have maintained their peace of mind when they have the same circumstances we **think** are causing us to feel awful.

Judgments

This is just forgetting about separate realities, and deluding ourselves into *thinking* our reality is the right one. For everything we judge, someone else has been able to *see* the same event with compassion and understanding. Judgment is similar to the pot calling the kettle black, or *looking for the mote in the eye of another, when the beam in our own eye distorts our view.* Those who *see* with compassion and understanding experience peace of mind. Those who judge, usually experience negative feelings within themselves, and blame it on whatever or whomever they are judging.

Judgment is an indicator of our own lostness rather than the lostness of the person we are judging. The person we are judging may be *lost* in thought-produced insecurity, which is taking the form of some kind of negativity. However, if we were not lost, we would *see* the innocence and know that person just doesn't know any better. We would feel compassion and understanding instead of judgment. Then we might be inspired to do something to make that person feel more secure, or we might get out of the way without judgment.

Expectations

Whenever we narrow our vision to expecting certain outcomes, we greatly increase the probability of disappointment. Then we wonder why we live in disappointment so much when our expectations are so wonderful. Beauty can be right in front of us, and be better than what we think we want, but we miss it when we are focused on expectations.

Assumptions

Assuming we know what someone else is thinking or experiencing is really a joke. We have missed a deep understanding of separate realities when we give credibility to our assumptions. When we base our own thoughts and feelings on our assumptions about what someone else thinks and feels, we react to our assumptions and blame others for what we think they think. It is humorous when we *see* it.

BELIEFS AND REALITIES

Ideas have no meaning except the meaning we give them. We attach such importance to the meaning we assign to our thoughts and ideas that they become beliefs which we live and die for.

A firm belief that the world is flat does not make it so. Believing water is clear because we can't see the microorganisms does not mean they are not there.

Another key to happiness is remembering that beliefs and realities are creations of our thoughts. When we forget this, our creations will seem very real to us. But when we recognize them for what they are -- just our way of seeing things for the moment -- we won't be bound by them.

GRATITUDE

Joe, "I can't see anything to be grateful for in this messed up world."

Wise old Zeke, "I'll bet you would be a millionaire if I told you I would give you $100 for everything you could think of to be grateful for."

Gratitude is a natural feeling when negative thoughts have been dismissed. The beauty of life is all around us. In higher levels of consciousness we *see* the beauty and are filled with gratitude. When filled with gratitude we *see* clearly how silly it is to be upset by some of the little things we take seriously in a lower state of mind.

When first learning about the principles I felt disappointed in myself every time I got lost in thought. As my understanding increased I didn't take this seriously and had compassion for myself. Now I even feel a sense of gratitude when I get lost because I know I will come out of it with greater understanding. Every time I get off track and experience my judgments or any other form of negativity, it confirms that it is not a pleasant place to be, and my under - standing deepens. You can imagine how much more pleasant lostness is when feeling gratitude instead of taking it seriously and judging it. The lostness keeps getting shorter and shorter.

It is impossible to feel gratitude and negativity at the same time. My *understanding* of that truth lets me know that it makes sense to focus on what I am grateful for, rather than what I have been thinking about to make myself unhappy. I sometimes catch myself in negative thought and start singing, *Oh What A Beautiful Morning*. Unhappiness is dismissed, and happiness comes flooding in.

COMPASSION

Feeling compassion is another natural occurance when we *see* what thought is. With perspective we *see* the innocence in everyone, and know that they do the very best they can from their present level of understanding.

When we have compassion, it is natural to forgive ourselves as well as others.

So much is missed when our focus is narrowed by the blinders of expectation, ego, and judgment.

BLINDERS

When I remove my blinders
the beauty of
  what is
    of life
    of you
    of me
is overwhelming

When I quit frustrating myself
  with expectations
    from life
    from you
    from myself

I am
  filled
  content
  at peace
    with my good fortune

When we dismiss the blinders of shoulds and rules, we allow ourselves to be guided by inspiration from our common sense and wisdom.

The blinder of ego is dismissed automatically with recognition -- at least until it sneaks back disguised in another thought. We can have quite a game of hide-and-seek with the illusion of ego.

WHAT WE SEE OR FEEL OR GIVE IS WHAT WE GET

When we are in a low mood and feeling judgmental or angry, we are stuck with those feelings. When we are in a high mood and *see* the innocence of all behavior, we have feelings of love, compassion, understanding and peace of mind. When we give love, that is what we get. We don't have to get it from someone else. Love is inherent in the feelings we have when we give love.

LOVE AND UNDERSTANDING

The greatest key of all is love. When we feel loving, we *see* beauty and positivity in everything. All that is needed to solve any problem we can imagine is love and understanding.

Love and understanding are the same thing. Love without understanding is conditional (not love at all.)

With understanding we see thought for what it is. With understanding, it is impossible to judge. With understanding we have compassion. With understanding we have peace of mind and contentment. With understanding we have beautiful feelings which will guide us to respond appropriately in every situation.

Another reminder that this is not about *shoulds*. Suppose you don't feel love and understanding? So what? What you feel is what you feel, based on your present level of understanding. *Shoulding* on yourself about that just makes it worse. Understanding usually changes what you feel, but if you try to change it through shoulds, you block understanding.

Just keep listening to your own wisdom until *understanding* sneaks past your thought system.

THE BATTLE BETWEEN LOVE AND EGO

Love is the ultimate reality. Ego is the ultimate illusion. Ego is the need to prove self-importance, which is based on the illusionary possibility of insecurity. It is the source of jealousy, self-righteousness, possessiveness, judgment, expectations of how things should be, revenge, depression, stress, and disease.

What power this illusion of ego can create.

Love has more power.

Love heals every problem. Through the perspective of love, problems disappear. Love fills us with feelings which guide us in solutions before we even think of them as solutions.

Joe chided Zeke, "All this talk of love sounds like religion and the flower children from the 60's to me. It really turns me off."

Wise old Zeke replied, "Could it be that the reason you don't have much love in your life is because it turns you off?"

ENJOYING WHAT IS WHILE IT IS

Have you ever had the experience of looking back at a time in your life and thought, "I was really happy then. Too bad I didn't realize it so I could have enjoyed it more."?

Have you known others who did not appreciate what they had until they lost it?

When we *understand* principles, the beauty of life is profound. What used to seem insignificant or taken for granted is seen with appreciation and gratitude. We are often so filled with beauty, contentment, and the wonder of life that we don't have any choice except to get quiet and enjoy it.

I got a glimpse of life today
beyond my thoughts
and was filled
with wonder
with beauty
with peace
and gratitude.

HAPPINESS AND PEACE OF MIND

What could be more important than happiness and peace of mind?

When happiness is what we want, it does not make sense to entertain thoughts that lead in any other direction.

Can you imagine the wonderful revolution that will take place when we all start laughing at the many silly thoughts which create so much misery?

It is so simple. **Dismiss negative thoughts and you have happiness and peace of mind.**

SUNRISE PRESS

ORDER FORM

Quantity orders will be allowed the following discount:

10-29 copies . . . . 20% discount
30-49 copies . . . . 30% discount
50 + copies . . . . 40% discount

To: SUNRISE PRESS   Phone (916) 961-5551
    4984 Arboleda Drive
    Fair Oaks, CA 95628

Please send the following:

_____ copies of *UNDERSTANDING:*
Eliminating Stress and Dissatisfaction in
Life and Relationships @ $7.95 $_____

_____ copies of *POSITIVE DISCIPLINE:*
Teaching Children Self-discipline,
Responsibility, Cooperation, and
Problem-solving Skills @ $7.95 $_____

_____ Set of ten black & white glossy posters
(17 x 22) of illustrations in Positive
Discipline (for study groups) $10.00 $_____

California Residents add 6% sales tax $_____

Shipping and handling 75¢ 1st book   _____

25¢ each additional book   _____

$2.00 shipping and handling for posters   _____

TOTAL $_____

_____ Please send information on lectures and workshops.

METHOD OF PAYMENT (Check One):

☐ Check or Money Order PAYABLE TO SUNRISE PRESS enclosed
Charge my ☐ MASTERCARD   ☐ VISA

_____   _____
Charge Card Account Number   "Good Through" or Expiration Date

_____
Signature of authorized buyer

Ship to _____

Address_____

City _____ State_____Zip_____